Flowdreaming

Audio Programs by Summer McStravick

Flowdreaming for Enhanced Creativity and Success

Flowdreaming for Happy Relationships

Flowdreaming for Immediate Relief

*Flowdreaming for Lots of Money, a Great Job,
and a Luxury Lifestyle*

Flowdreaming for Perfect Physical and Mental Health

Please visit Hay House USA: www.hayhouse.com®
Hay House Australia: www.hayhouse.com.au
Hay House UK: www.hayhouse.co.uk
Hay House South Africa: orders@psdprom.co.za
Hay House India: www.hayhouseindia.co.in

Flowdreaming

A Radical New Technique for Manifesting
Anything You Want

Summer McStravick

HAY HOUSE, INC.
Carlsbad, California
London • Sydney • Johannesburg
Vancouver • Hong Kong • Mumbai

Published and distributed in the United States by: Hay House, Inc.: www.hayhouse.com •
Published and distributed in Australia by: Hay House Australia Pty. Ltd.: www.hayhouse.
com.au • **Published and distributed in the United Kingdom by:** Hay House UK, Ltd.: www.
hayhouse.co.uk • **Published and distributed in the Republic of South Africa by:** Hay House SA
(Pty), Ltd.: orders@psdprom.co.za • **Distributed in Canada by:** Raincoast: www.raincoast.com
• **Published in India by:** Hay House Publications (India) Pvt. Ltd.: www.hayhouseindia.co.in •
Distributed in India by: Media Star: booksdivision@mediastar.co.in

Editorial supervision: Jill Kramer • *Design:* Charles McStravick

Library of Congress Control Number: 2005933489

ISBN 13: 978-1-4019-0561-3
ISBN 10: 1-4019-0561-7

09 08 07 06   4 3 2 1
1st printing, March 2006

Printed in the United States of America

To my mother, Venus Andrecht,
whose considerable knowledge, constant optimism,
and general doggedness has helped shape my life.
I couldn't have chosen a better family to be born into.
Without her partnership in creating the Flowdreaming
process, it would never have come to be.

And to my husband, Charles,
for his support and for giving me my
"Writing Sundays," and whose natural skepticism
keeps me balanced.

Contents

Introduction

W**e've always known that the Flow is all around us.** On some intuitive level, we feel its presence and know when we're moving with life, just as we recognize when we're moving against it. And on rare occasions—though just often enough to shake us up each time it happens—when we look at a sunset or up at the stars, we can even sense that we're *part of the Flow;* that is, made from the stuff. The Flow is both the glue that holds the cosmos together *and* the cosmos itself.

If you have any doubt about this, just think of how often you've used the expression "Just go with the flow."

Every time you've been moved to use that phrase, you've acknowledged, perhaps instinctually, that there is some life force—some peculiar essence—that we're caught up in and that is flowing forward into the future, and that, if we go with it, will ease our burdens and bring us to a better place. We intuit that this essence is good and pure, and we *want* to be flowing with it. In other words, when we're going with the Flow, we're saying that we are in fact on the right path . . . whatever that path may be.

The Flow can be understood as a great river, a coursing cosmic stream of creation that imbues everything it touches with life force. As the great American poet and thinker Ralph Waldo Emerson once observed: "Place yourself in the middle of the stream of power and wisdom which animates all whom it floats, and you are without effort impelled to truth, to right, and a perfect contentment."

Was Emerson referring to the Flow? Without a doubt.

Carl Jung, the preeminent psychologist and founder of Jungian therapy, also had a profound sense of the Flow. Consider this statement he once made: "At times I feel as if I am spread out over the landscape and inside things, and am myself living in every tree, in the splashing of the waves, in the clouds and the animals that come and go, in the procession of the seasons."

And certainly today, people continue to sense and write about the presence of the Flow. Some of us view the Flow from a spiritual vantage point as a great river of dynamic, creative universal energy, alive with consciousness and spirit (we may call it *tao, ki, prana, life essence,* and so forth), while others see it from a scientific perspective as a primordial energy field, one of infinite possibilities alive with quantum forces that are barely understood (the zero-point field, the elusive "theory of everything," and so on).

Still others sense the Flow through a lens of personal intimacy, wherein it's just another name for God: a sentient, compassionate, loving force that both permeates all things and is all things, for aren't all things both *from* and *of* God? Does God ever work with materials that haven't come from Itself? To say yes would mean that someone else created them . . . and we know that isn't true. So everything we touch and experience is quite literally a piece of God energy, whether it's the paper in this book you're holding now or a beautiful mountain range seen outside your window. It's all just a physical expression of a piece of God's primordial energy—as remarkable as that is to think about. So when you purposefully and consciously make yourself aware of this energy (or this energetic state), you're simply becoming aware of the flowing stream of God.

Contemporary novelist Joni Rodgers wrote this striking observation about prayer, which captures the essence of this understanding of the Flow: "Many people think they don't know how to pray. Just think of God as a great river that runs through the universe. The idea of prayer is not to pull God out of the stream but to put yourself into the stream with God."

However we choose to understand it, let us say, then, that the Flow is *all* of these things. It wears a coat of many colors, so that each of us looking through the kaleidoscope sees it in a way that becomes meaningful to us. Even atheists who marvel at the beauty and complexity of our reality connect with the Flow where they place their faith at the scientific level— because the Flow is whatever we sense as being the underpinning for the life and beauty in our world and our galaxy. It's all the same thing, but seen through different lenses.

What I'm going to show you now is how you can start aligning yourself with this majesty, and in so doing discover the explosive, creative, manifestational power that is the Flow.

CHAPTER ONE

How I Found the Flow

"**M**om," I said, "I feel terrible. It's like I'm knocking my head against the wall. I've been working seven days a week on this business, and nothing is happening—my magazine is going nowhere. I need your help."

On the other end of the phone, my mother, Venus, was trying to console me from her brightly decorated home in the mountains of Southern California. Mom has been a psychic counselor to countless people, practicing her unique gift of "clear-seeing" for more than 30 years.

I desperately needed her help. I didn't require any psychic insight, though—what I needed was *manifesting* energy. I needed to make things happen in my business, which seemed like a black hole that sucked more and more of my time for less and less income.

"Do you have time to go out there with me right now?" I asked.

"All right," my mother said. "Do you want to do it like always?"

"No, let's try something different. I have an idea . . . just follow me as I talk us through it."

Mom and I both closed our eyes as we held the phones to our ears, and I began talking us into a new place that neither of us had ever been to before.

For a while now, I'd been spending time each day doing creative visualization, in which I saw and felt the things I wanted to have happen in my life. It's an old idea (going back to the 1800s), and the gist of it is that you close your eyes and see exactly what you want to have in your life. You're not praying; rather, you're seeing and feeling exactly what you want and acting as if you *already have* whatever it is you desire. If you add positive affirmations, you can strengthen your creative visualization even more. Today people talk about making a "vibratory match" with whatever they desire, and keeping their thoughts in vibratory alignment with their goals.

Anyway, I'd been tinkering with these ideas for years, merging and blending them with something we'd been doing in my family my entire life. I knew that my mom went to a special "place" during clear-seeing by lifting her mind above everything (similar to the state spoken of in Buddhist thought), and from this "void" she was able to zero in on exactly the person you asked her to see. This could be anyone at all, anywhere in the world—all she needed was a first and last name. Like a plane flying at high altitude, her perspective changed, so she could find anyone from her vantage point. Having found them, she then allowed her mind to "touch" theirs, and after asking permission, she could enter into their thoughts and ask questions. It was a very unusual talent, and she'd passed on the fundamentals to me.

So, during my tinkering, I'd decided to try adding her technique of "going to the void" to the creative visualization I was doing—in essence, merging the two to see what I got. As I held the phone to my ear that day, I began talking both my mother and myself through what I'd thought was going to be just an interesting variation on visualization.

I began by sensing the energy around my body as a vibrating, living field. I imagined this in my mind, but I also coaxed myself into *physically* feeling what it would be like if I were indeed surrounded by humming, vibrational energy. Then I mentally dissolved this energy into that of the world around me—in effect merging my own energy with it—so I couldn't sense any distinction between my own energy and that of everything surrounding me. I allowed myself to actually feel this taking place, using my own creativity to get it going. Interestingly, as I did so, I sensed that this energy was moving in a particular way: a forward, distinct direction. I allowed my body to actually sway forward, unabashedly giving my whole self over to the experience.

Then I directed both Mom and myself to sense this energy spreading out into the world—streaking across the sky, through the atmosphere. I mentally "felt" my mind expanding at an enormous rate, touching everything. I saw all of this in my mind like a daydream—one I was purposely guiding with my thoughts. Next I directed us to look for that special void so that we could begin visualizing what we wanted from that location.

"Do you see that?" I asked my mother as I reached that place. "I see something, but I'm not sensing *your* void. I'm seeing this whirling, sparkling mass out there."

She paused a moment, then said, "I'm going to see a door in my mind, then open it with the idea that I will be where you are." A few seconds went by, then she said, "Okay, I see this energy, too."

But I'd already plunged my mind into the energy to see what it was. I discovered that it was moving and flowing, much like a great river. "It's moving forward like rapids, Mom," I said. "I can feel myself being carried with it. It's a great, flowing river of energy."

"I see it, too," she echoed. "It's going somewhere. Look ahead and tell me what you see."

I did so, telling her, "I'm getting a picture." I watched as an image of a rope ladder formed in my mind. I told her what I was seeing and asked her what she thought it meant.

"It sounds like a rough way to go," she answered.

"Yeah, but that's what I see."

At once I connected this image with what I'd been intending to manifest out there: positive progress and money for my business. "I think I'm getting a message that this business of mine is like a rope ladder," I explained. "It's a tough climb."

"Why don't you change it, then?" she challenged me.

In my mind, I "erased" the rope ladder and instead saw a wide bank of creamy marble steps, the kind you'd see in front of a grand library. *That's more like it,* I thought. *If I have any climbing to do, I want to make it easy and elegant.*

"Why make steps at all?" Mom suggested. "I'd visualize an escalator."

Of course! This time, together we felt a smooth escalator moving me up effortlessly into the sky, with the escalator being a symbol for the easy rise of success in my business.

We then both opened our eyes and came out of the experience and began excitedly going over the details. We both admitted that it had felt completely different from anything we'd done before. It was, in fact, my earliest, fumbling experience in the Flow.

What we discovered that day was that there exists a "place" accessible in our minds, where you seem to "hook in" to an energetic, cosmic river that flows in a positive direction. The image of it as a river is the way our minds interpret what's inherently too big to fully understand, so it comes to us as metaphoric imagery.

I've since experimented and gone into deeper levels of this place, where the Flow becomes a sparkling, swirling mass of energy held together by iridescent cosmic threads of light, all woven together in intricate patterns. Each strand of light is its own Flow, where the smaller Flows of events and thoughts and people come together to form the flowing patterns of energetic interaction in my life. By reconfiguring the pattern, like a knitter who directs the patterns of stitches in a scarf, you can likewise change and guide these energetic Flows before they manifest as physical reality in your life.

So from this surprising, exploratory beginning, what has since become abundantly clear are a few remarkable things:

1. The Flow can be accessed by anyone.

2. It will show itself differently to everyone, since we all come to it with our own unique understanding.

3. The Flow is a place of great harmonizing and manifesting power.

4. It always travels in a particular, forward direction that mirrors the forward movement of life.

5. It feels outside of time and space.

6. Every thought, event, action, object, and situation in life has its very own personal Flow, which is part and parcel of this larger Flow.

7. You can easily access the Flow by utilizing what I've come to know as "Flowdreaming," which is simply a technique used to get there and start making things happen in this great energetic space.

Now let's explore what Flowdreaming is in a bit more depth.

CHAPTER TWO

What Is the Flow?

To understand the Flow more completely, we need to talk *body, mind,* and *spirit* for a moment—namely, where they all are. So let's do an easy thought experiment right now. Stop reading and take a look at your hand. Look hard.

You know that your hand is made up of tissue, blood, and bones. If you remember your high school or college biology class, you might also realize that these materials are each made of tiny cells, which are in turn made of minute proteins that are constructed from DNA and RNA . . .

which are themselves made from molecules . . . which are made of individual atoms . . . which come from—what? What comes next?

Squint now and pretend that you're seeing your hand down at its most basic level. It's not solid at all, is it? Note how there's so much space between the atoms. Do you remember hearing that your hand is mostly empty space, that you only see it as solid because the atoms are so tightly packed together that it gives the *illusion* of solidity—just like when you look at a cloud it appears solid, even though you know it's not?

So then what's in between those atoms? Nothing? Empty space? Is that *really* what you're made of? Does that feel right to you? Your gut probably says no, yet because this is a difficult thing to think about, you may feel like leaving this subject right here. *Good enough,* you might figure. *Who cares what I'm made of? I have a body and a spirit, and who cares how they're joined together. When I die, my soul will float free—okay, so I guess that means it's anchored to me somehow, but I sure don't know where it is now. All I know is that even though I don't actually know where my soul is, I'd better be good anyway because the things I do in this body affect my soul.*

Here's a surprise: While you think that your religious upbringing has taught you this belief, the fact is that no matter what your faith or philosophical perspective, you've probably been more influenced by Western scientific/philosophic culture, which teaches you to believe in the doctrine of *dualism*.

Dualism means that there are two realms of existence: one of the material world and physicality, and one of spirit or soul. Since you were a child, you've been taught that your mind is located in your body; while your spirit, or some greater soul self, is completely separate, existing in some other place away from your body. In other words, your soul and your body occupy completely different realms. They're divorced from one another and, frankly, not on speaking terms.

So whatever is in that empty space past the physical matter in your hand is something you might figure out when you die—when God explains it all—but until then, your brain is in your body, your mind is your brain (which is where all your thinking goes on and where you get your sense of you are), and your soul is somewhere else entirely.

Of course you know that the brain in your head, the part of you that's reading right now, isn't *all* you are.

Somehow your soul, your individuality, does get through (because that's what makes each of us unique, right?), but you sure can't find out where the connection is taking place. After all, there's no organ about which doctors say, "Ah, this is your soul receiver. It takes the signals in here and descrambles them for you here and gives you your unique selfhood."

Many biologists and cognitive scientists go a step further and are all too willing to demand, "Forget that soul business altogether! You're nothing except a bunch of learned behaviors and a soup of peptides and molecules. There's no spirit there—it's an illusion. Self-awareness, or that sense of who you are, is just a biological accident . . . a side effect, as it were, that evolution found useful."

Even if you feel that sentiment is wrong because your faith or spirituality tells you otherwise, you're probably still baffled as to where your soul is—that part of yourself that makes you uniquely *you*. That's why it's easiest to shrug it off and say that it's out there somewhere, in another realm. And that's dualism.

So what's wrong with this old dualistic way of thinking?
Well, it's just not working for us anymore. Science has in fact moved ahead, and all of us regular folk are just starting

to catch up in our thinking. To even have thoughts about these things right now means that you're ahead of the curve—probably by a hundred years or so. That's how long it will take the next few generations to start catching up to these ideas on a mass level.

For now, most people are still stuck in this dualist way of thinking that's based on an understanding of the world put forward by René Descartes, who first proposed these "two realms" of existence (known as the "Cartesian split"), in the 1600s. Does it make sense that this 400-year-old vision has finally broken down under the scrutiny of today's quantum physics?

Today we're discovering that mind (or soul) and matter are becoming much harder to keep separate. In fact, the more we try to keep them apart, the more they seem to want to work together. Of course, for hundreds of years, Spiritualists and other forward-thinking groups have been suggesting that mind and matter are really made of the same invisible stuff—they aren't split apart at all, it's just our limited perception of them that leads us to think that. The idea is that, just like when we stick our finger in a pool of water and see the ripples moving away, when we think something, it can't help but affect the matter (the world) around us. Mind and matter are inseparable: Every thought we have disturbs the physical world around it in one way or another . . . for good or ill.

"Oh, right," say the old-guard scientists, "your mind is only good for *observing* the matter around you. You can look at and think about things, but until you reach out and physically touch something, it can't really *affect* it."

"Not so," retort a surprising group of new scientists, from physics professors to mathematicians to biologists. A growing number are saying, "Your mind affecting your world—even creating your world—wouldn't really contradict the laws of science after all, since these laws are evolving right under our noses . . . in fact, it helps explain a lot of things!"

Like what? Premonition, intuition, and luck, for starters. And how "like attracts like" *and* "opposites attract." And how you "know" when certain things will happen and when they won't. It's how your dog knows to be waiting for you when you walk in the door, and how "the strangest coincidences" occur in your life. It's how being near a healthy, positive person can cause an ill person to get well—or vice versa. It's how you suddenly think of your friend the minute the phone rings, and it is indeed this person calling.

This means that the "two realms" theory—the mind/body split—is going the way of the dinosaur. Today we've begun talking about the zero-point field, multidimensional space, morphogenic fields, and synchronicity. And for this little thought experiment, the most important thing is a new way of looking at *your own* mind.

So what does any of this have to do with the Flow?

Well, now I'd like you to prepare yourself to think something new, something completely different from your usual idea of the world, and perhaps even of spirit and God. Let's experiment with a new way of thinking about your body, mind, and soul.

In this model, your entire self is like a string of musical notes, from the lowest to the highest. So high and so low, in fact, that you can't sense where they begin or end. You can hear some of these low notes, which make up your physical body, since they're made up of the atoms and molecules in your body. But now let's go up the scale. The midtones are your mind—do you hear their sounds? All day long the tones of your vibrational self manifest as the mental you through thoughts, inspiration, dreams, breakthroughs, déjà vu, and the like. And the highest notes, the ones that are just out of your hearing (because, after all, the lowest notes of your body only have a limited spectrum that they can "hear") are your soul.

In other words, you exist at this very moment in a number of energy locations, all the way up the octave, so to speak. Your body and brain are in one, but right on top of that is another energetic level of you: your true mind, the one that exists outside of your physical self. And next to that is another energy level: your soul, which extends through many frequencies *ad infinitum*. But they exist all at once, altogether. From your current physical perspective, you can use one (your body), have limited access to another (your true mind), and only contemplate the existence of the last (your soul).

Another metaphor for your body, mind, and soul is a continuum of frequencies. Frequencies are simply measurements of waves. As University of Oregon physics professor Amit Goswami puts it, frequencies are simply "how fast a wave [of energy] wiggles." Just about everything can be measured in terms of these wiggles. For example, light frequencies make up both visible and invisible spectrums of wave energy. This means that you can see red light as the color red, but you can't see the ultraviolet light that gives you a sunburn. Sound also travels in frequencies: Dogs pick up noises that we can't, and our radios and cell phones pick up frequencies that are around us all the time—all through the air—yet we can't hear. So just because our puny physical bodies are biologically incapable of sensing a frequency doesn't mean that it doesn't exist.

In fact, we've made all kind of machines that help us see and hear these frequencies that our biological brains can't, such as cell phones, radios, and satellite TVs. Our machines are picking up frequencies that our bodies can't detect on their own. We're figuratively swimming in a bath of frequencies right now: Think about the billions of cell-phone conversations going on around us, the TV signals flooding the air around us, and the radio stations bombarding us. No wonder we feel so overwhelmed all the time—the air around us is extremely busy with information . . . not to mention cosmic waves and other natural sources of energy that are also everywhere around us.

My point is that our physical bodies are very limited in perceiving frequency spectrums or wave energy. But because we can't hear or see them doesn't mean that, say, TV signals don't exist. In fact, all objects in our solar system are made of wave energy (wiggles) at their source. You are, I am, and so is the book you're looking at right now. All things in the Universe are simply different "tunings" of this energy.

Think of yourself as an individual stream, or flow, of energy, and this book as another stream. Now think of *everything* around you as individual streams of energy. Think of the room you're in as a pattern or stream of energy: Everything inside this room is both separate from the room, but within it at the same time. That is, you're both part of and separate from the room around you. This is how flows of energy interact with one another—they're both separate from and part of everything else. If you grasp that concept, you're well on the way to understanding the Flow!

You see, just by virtue of existing, you're participating in the universal Flow right now, at this very moment. You're part of the layer upon layer upon layer of Flow—ending up in the Source Pool of the Flow itself. You're both separate from and part of this Source, just as an object in a room is both separate from and part of that room. Your personal Flow and the Flows of everything you're interacting with are mixing and colliding with each other right now. This includes your thoughts and those of other people, the frequencies of light and color around you *and* of the electrons spinning in every physical object surrounding you. This, interestingly, leads us right back to your hand. Can you see what's in the empty spaces between those atoms now? Yes, it's the Flow—the radiant energy of all things, which is ultimately stored as wave information.

If you take anything at all away from these last few paragraphs, take this: You're *way* bigger than you think. In fact, you go far beyond your body—your physical shell is just the very edge of the Greater You, like the skin of an orange. Your consciousness exists in all the levels of your selfhood, yet from this little physical Flow (or body) that you're in right now, you feel cut off from the rest of the Greater You, because your body is physically limited from experiencing these higher frequencies, or Flows.

So what I'm asking you to do now is instead of seeing your body, mind, and soul as three separate and distinct things, think of them as gradations of energy along a vast spectrum, existing simultaneously along the Flow continuum of energy. These "yous" exist on finer and finer levels—from the outside, visible you (your body) to the finer, invisible you (your mind and spirit)—and your consciousness is a bridge between them. This means that instead of being "somewhere else," your soul is here with you right now. Your mind and your soul are existing *together* right now, not a hair's width away from one another. You're only aware of a small portion of this Greater You—the portion that your little biological brain was evolved to sense—and that's your body and the inkling of self-awareness that your brain possesses.

A good analogy is to think about your hand again. What if that hand said, "A hand is all that I am. I think I could be connected to something else, but I don't know what. It's funny, though: Sometimes I feel like I'm being directed or guided—I find myself in situations and wonder how I got here. It's like some situations I encounter were set up for me."

The hand would be quite right—the Greater You is the one doing the real thinking. It's placing the hand into the situations that It thinks is best for the hand so that It can create experiences using the hand, even though the hand isn't aware of the rest of the "body" doing all this. You can see your conscious self as the hand, and your "body" as the Greater You. The Greater You puts you where you need to be.

The biggest lesson to get here is that you are everything at once: your body, mind, and soul. They don't exist separate from one another; in other words, your soul isn't in hiding somewhere—it's simply out of your biological "hearing" range. Your soul is aware of everything, your mind is aware of some things, and your body is aware of the least of all. Unfortunately, because we're alive, the body has the dominant perspective. Its biological drives, its genetic composition, even its sex create the filter to the world that we must act through. But fortunately, our *mind* is there to bridge the gap.

You see, during your day, your consciousness is both present in your brain and is receiving a huge amount of information from the part of itself that exists in the Flow—that is, in these finer vibratory frequencies. In other words, your mind exists both within and outside of your brain. You could say that it's literally in two places at once—in both the physical self and the nonphysical, quantum self. Your brain acts as a terrific filtering, processing, and storage device: It takes in loads of information, both consciously and subconsciously, processes it, interprets it, draws conclusions from it, and stores it. Most of the time, the decisions you make are coming from your brain, but at the same time, your quantum mind is accessing all this same information, as is your soul. Your mind—and by that I mean those thought processes that are happening at the quantum level—is bridging the vibrational divide between your body and soul.

Through the vehicle of your mind, you move up and down in vibrational access throughout the day—sometimes your brain is dominant, while other times you move into higher levels of yourself to make decisions and process information. When you're angry, for instance, your biological brain is operating with 100 percent authority. But when you're in a meditative state or a focused, blissful place where you lose track of time (creative people often report this state), you've moved up the spectrum into another level of being—one that is more blended between your brain, mind, and soul. You can think of an old-fashioned thermometer in which the red line indicates higher temperatures: *Your* red line moves up and down this gauge all day long as you access different levels of yourself for different purposes. Every time you think, you're moving in and out of these finer fields at a quantum level.

Bringing this back to the Flow, when you purposely move into this state of awareness—the Flow state—you're moving into and aligning yourself more firmly within life's finer energy fields, where reality takes shape at its most basic level. Flowdreaming allows you to expand your access to these finer fields, where the world as we know it is first thought into reality.

If you'd like to learn more about the science behind the Flow, please skip to Chapter 7 of this book. The material is a little more complicated, but well worth exploring. For now, though, we're going right to the part where you can learn how to use the Flow to start making changes in your life, as you access the greatest manifesting power ever.

CHAPTER THREE

Preparing to Flowdream

Flowdreaming is incredibly easy. There's almost nothing to learn, since you already essentially know how to do it. Here I'm just going to offer you a tour guide's view of the Flow, giving you pointers to make your journey easier, along with images and processes to make your experience with it most useful.

To start, imagine the Flow as a "place" you access through your imagination. After all, what is imagination but consciousness? And if consciousness is already adrift in the Flow, then your imagination is already existing there, too, at least to some degree. So you're not really traveling at all—you're already in the Flow just by virtue of thinking! Nevertheless, it helps to have pictures you can use to "see" this space so that when you're feeling or visualizing yourself there, you'll have a concrete image to relate to.

You can see the Flow as a sparkling, warm, buoyant stream, or it can be a flowing cascade of iridescent cosmic energy—either way, imagine it as traveling under, through, around, and behind our normal 3-D reality. Visualize the Flow as a place where patterns are born and where both synchronicity and synergism hold sway. You can imagine our physical reality and Flow reality as being like twin strands of string woven together to make the same cloth, so impacting the one impacts the other. By affecting the fine substance (Flow), you affect the gross substance (material reality)—so by changing the molecules, water becomes wine.

It doesn't matter what form you give it—what's important is that when you go into the Flow (for the moment, at least), you believe that it exists, and that, as a part of it, you can participate in and direct it. In order to Flowdream, you must combine vivid, saturated imagery with strong, purposeful emotion. In this daydream (Flowdream), you go to this "place" outside of time or space—the Flow—where your mind and your desires become participatory, creative forces that can actively alter the circumstances in your life. In other words, while in the Flow, you see and, most important, *feel* those things you want to have happen, and that's what will manifest in your life.

YOUR LIFE HAS ITS OWN FLOW

Let's start with your personal Flow. To get the most out of this process, you need to become comfortable with a series of ideas. Whether you believe them completely or not doesn't seem to matter, as long as you can suspend your disbelief while you're Flowdreaming.

Being in the Flow assumes the following:

1. The Flow is a creative, manifestational field or cosmic consciousness that you're a part of, and from this "place" you can participate in directing your life through thought alone.

2. Your particular Flow moves, or *flows,* in a general direction toward order and evolution, which also means your highest good and happiness.

3. When you fight against the current of your Flow, you create obstacles and frustration—things stop going your way.

4. Guided daydreaming or "Flowdreaming," coupled with strong emotion, can take you into your Flow.

5. Once in the Flow, you can start manifesting those things you want to occur in your life, and they *will* start to happen as long as they fit well with your Flow and the Flow of those around you. If they don't fit in, either you'll find yourself swimming against the current if you continue to stay fixated on those things, or those particular desires simply won't manifest—something even better and more in keeping with your Flow will come to you instead.

The second point in this list is particularly important. The Flow is not a disorganized, chaotic, wholly entropic place; instead, it's subtly governed by some of the same natural laws that rule the Universe. Consider how all natural phenomena have cycles and seasons, moving from birth to death, from spring to summer and fall to winter. Plants sprout, grow, and die; water evaporates up from the ocean, turns to rain, and falls back to the sea. These directional cycles always flow in one direction—that is, spring never turns to winter, people never grow younger, and streams never flow backward. The Universe is always expanding, not contracting.

If you extend this out, then you can apply value judgments to these processes. In other words, when you flow *with* a current, it's "easy" and requires little expenditure of energy; while when you swim *against* the current, it's "hard" and requires vastly more effort. When birds fly, they do so *with* the air currents. As a result, they go farther and faster, and experience a "better" life, than those birds who beat their wings against the airflows (if any such birds exist!). As people, we tend to equate *easy* and *natural* with *good* and *progressive*.

If you apply this idea to your own life, you can see that it has followed a similar pattern, albeit with many more complexities. You've tended to consider the times when you've "flowed with the current" as having been positive, good experiences. For example, you can probably recall times when everything was working out for you. Everything was easy, and things seemed to effortlessly fall into place. The popular phrase "Go with the flow" has its roots in this idea.

This brings us to the third point on the list: When you fight against the current of your Flow, you create obstacles and frustration. Things stop "going your way." You can probably also identify points in your life where you felt that no matter what you did, you were "blocked." The energy you expended was wasted, and one difficulty after another was thrown up before you. If you persisted and ultimately achieved your desires anyway, you still felt that it was "an uphill battle."

I include these well-worn phrases on purpose, to show that we've all had a sense of these currents running through our lives. And most of us, if given a choice, would opt for going with the Flow rather than against it. We want to attract or manifest those things that add to the positive, easy processes in our lives. That's a core idea of Flowdreaming.

As the name implies, Flowdreaming means accessing your Flow (the cosmic consciousness, manifestational field, and so on) through focused, guided daydreaming (the fourth point on the aforementioned list). Daydreaming just happens to be a form of consciousness that's easy and natural, and it offers a simple way to access your Flow because it's something you already know how to do and brings you to an altered state of mind.

In fact, that's the reason the Flow works so well and so quickly for people—daydreaming is something everyone already knows how to do. There's very little learning curve, so you can just get right in and start making things happen in your life.

Daydreaming, like dreaming at night, is an essential part of living. However, remarkably little research has been done with daydreaming, leaving its function in our lives wide open to interpretation. The few studies that have been conducted have focused either on where or how a daydream occurs or on content (such as its Freudian aspects). Even the true function of night dreaming (what it actually does for us), which has been extensively studied, has yet to be determined.

So it's possible to suggest that daydreaming is in fact very similar to night dreaming. This would mean that when daydreaming is stifled, the mind becomes stressed, and concentration on other tasks becomes increasingly difficult. Healthy daydreaming, therefore, is critical to life.

Consider what it already does for you: (1) It gives constant, subtle course corrections to your waking reality; (2) it directs you toward your goals; and (3) it subtly assesses and corrects earlier behaviors, like an on-the-fly mental review by your subconscious.

Common experience shows that most people's daydreams often center around "should have/could have" situations in which a person emerges as a hero by either remaking a scene that went poorly for them at some earlier point or by creating an entirely new scenario. For instance, you might find yourself saying "I *should have* told her that I wanted to see my friends because it's important for me to maintain those relationships, instead of that I didn't want to see *her*."

You might accompany this by seeing the scene that happened earlier in your mind, then actually saying the new, corrected dialogue in your mind. (And the pathological counterpart to this kind of daydream is when the person simply replays the guilt-ridden or anxiety-producing situation without a correcting episode.)

Another common scenario is the future- or goal-oriented daydream, in which you create a mini-movie of a situation or conversation you want to have happen. By rehearsing it in your mind, you mentally prep yourself for the oncoming event, which might be anything from a conversation with your boss to asking someone out on a date to envisioning a trip to Hawaii. Please note that there's a tremendous difference between this kind of daydreaming and Flowdreaming—the former is more like its watered-down cousin.

Yet another common daydream is the to-do list: You might be planning out the rest of your day, in order, and juggling around appointments and chores. This must be differentiated from *consciously* going through your to-do list, where you actually plan what to do and where you're going— the daydreaming to-do list is more free-flowing as you add things to it, then cross them off, rearrange them, and throw in a good half-dozen purely extraneous chores that you won't even consider doing anytime soon . . . and what's more, at some point you "come back to reality" to discover that you somehow drifted off and half your list has been lost.

What's important to note about all of these types of daydreams is that your conscious mind is usually only half aware of what it's doing when in the midst of one. It's as if your mind is running these daydreams in the background of other conscious actions. You might be driving while they take place, or in the shower—or you could be sitting in front of your computer at work when you suddenly realize that your attention has been elsewhere for some time. Your mind actually takes many side trips like these throughout the day whenever it's not fully engaged in a demanding mental activity.

Usually, at some point in any of these reveries, something will bring you back to reality, and your daydream will be abruptly cut off . . . sometimes without your even realizing you were having one! If it was interrupted and the scene was incomplete, there's a good chance that your mind will return to it in order to finish it at another time. (Hence, recurring daydreams.)

So Flowdreaming, which is a kind of guided daydreaming, is only a little bit different from what you're already used to. However, instead of waking up in the middle of your reverie to find your mind rehashing a situation, you instead consciously decide to embark on a daydream and then direct the images in your mind. The Flow aspect is what causes the daydream to extend outward beyond your own mind, to become an effective, creative, manifestational process. You can imagine yourself as traveling "up" the vibratory rope of your daydream into the Flow as your mind moves from one state of consciousness to another, as you use your daydream as a key to unlock the door to the cosmic manifestational field.

"But What If I Don't Daydream?"

A few nights ago my husband told me that he hasn't daydreamed since he was a teenager. I asked, "So what do you consider to be a daydream?"

It turns out that he thought it meant kicking back with a soda and thinking about what you were going to be someday, like the adolescent fantasy of being a rock star wowing 'em onstage.

I had to laugh. Then I asked if he ever caught himself mentally prepping for a situation at the publishing house where he works. "Don't you see your desk and the book you're working on in your mind?" I queried. "Then you see yourself calling the author to discuss a point or maybe try a few phrases out in your head, when suddenly you're back in traffic on the freeway?"

"Well, yeah," he said, "but that's just being lost in thought."

"So lost in thought, where you're literally *lost* to the present, isn't a form of daydreaming?" I continued. "You certainly aren't *aware* of being lost in thought—your mind has checked out for a few minutes without telling you. And what is it doing? It's seeing, hearing, ruminating, and thoroughly going over a fantasy situation in your mind."

He got the point.

So maybe you should also reconsider what *you* think of daydreaming if you're having trouble with the idea. As with visualization, people sometimes feel confused about what they're doing, not because they're doing it wrong, but because they're afraid that what they're doing might be different from what others are doing. I've heard people admit that they expect to see 3-D reality while visualizing, and when they fall short, they moan that they "just can't do it."

Anyone could tell these individuals that we all fall in a spectrum in our visualizing abilities. It's something that's impossible to quantify. How can you tell if your daydream is more "real" or developed than someone else's? You can't. So just let your mind "go natural" and fall into the way you usually daydream. It knows what it's doing, and it will go there. It's just like breathing: When you focus too hard on your inhalations and exhalations, you suddenly can't breathe evenly anymore!

Sometimes you have to work at daydreaming for a few minutes before your mind slides into this state. Remember that your mind usually drifts into daydreams without your conscious help, so now that you're guiding it along, it may feel foreign or weird for the first few minutes. But don't worry—that will change with practice.

Be happy if you experience one, two, or even a string of very vivid objects or scenes during your Flowdreaming. They may flash in your mind for a few seconds before morphing out of shape, and they might be followed by a strong sensation or a remembered smell. Your mind likes to "see" the way you do in dreams at night. Sometimes things are extremely vivid; others are more vague, but you still have a clear understanding of what they are. When you see someone in a nighttime dream, you often don't see actual facial features—and sometimes they "wear the body" of someone else entirely—but you have a clear idea of who they are. Or when you read a really engrossing novel, you create scenes in your head in which the characters enact the scenes on the page. Are you visualizing then? Yes. Is this incredibly similar to guided daydreaming? Absolutely.

The Power of Emotion

Reading is a great framework for thinking of this next critical point: *Flowdreaming requires emotion.* Anything you put into the Flow is magnified and energized by your feelings. Compare this to when you get caught up in a really engrossing story—your emotional connection is what makes the difference between a good book and a boring one. When you're following the text with scenes in your mind, you're also unconsciously infusing these scenes with emotion: fear, longing, joy, anticipation, and so on. You must bring this *same emotional connection* to your Flowdream.

Emotion is like an electrical charge that excites and supercharges the energy in the Flow. It's what propels your consciousness in the Flow, like gas propels your car. Imagine floating gently down the stream of your Flow . . . now imagine cruising in your emotion-powered motorboat. The more emotion you transmit in the Flow, the farther, faster, and more profoundly your desires will manifest. This is because emotion excites energy—*will*—which generates strong manifestational power. Your strong intention, or *desire,* is what drives the creative power of your Flow.

Flowdreaming should never be a dry intellectual exercise. If you can't summon emotion into your Flowdreaming, then I suggest that you play Track 2 on the CD ("Exercise 1: Your Emotional Self") over and over until summoning emotion feels totally natural.

In addition to sensing desire when in the Flow, also focus on feeling joy, gratitude, and thankfulness. This may be why praying works so well. You see, feeling thankfulness, as during prayer, is an *affirming* emotion—any such emotion creates a vibrational pattern that acknowledges that what you're manifesting is already coming true. So being thankful isn't merely a pious platitude; rather, feelings of love, awe, gratitude, and thankfulness carry *positive force*.

In addition, curiosity is another powerful emotion in the Flow—it can lead to undiscovered wonders revealing themselves in your life. Ask to learn more when you're in the Flow, since ultimately we're only tapping the smallest portion of what's out there. To think that we know it all is small-minded indeed.

Remember that being in the Flow without emotion is like throwing a ball underwater: It won't travel far. So let your feelings out!

YOUR EMOTIONAL SELF

As long as we're discussing emotions, have you ever thought about your relationship to your own emotions? We're all taught from early on that our emotions are inherently reactive—that is, we feel one way or another as a reaction to outside events and situations. In other words, we wait for events outside of us to determine our emotional states, keeping us at the mercy of other people and situations that we don't have control over. We're not the masters of our emotions; we're just the *receivers* of them, while situations buffet us around and make us feel one way or another.

What's more, we're expected to feel emotionally appropriate: "I'm so happy when you say you love me," "I'm so sad now that you're gone," "I'm angry because you cheated me," and "I'm heartbroken that I lost that job" are all examples of emotionally appropriate reactions. In every case, we're not the chooser of these feelings—other people have determined them for us, and we dutifully experience the expected emotion.

Furthermore, we're expected to react emotionally appropriate in every case. We can't be joyful when a tragedy occurs, nor can we be unhappy when we win the lottery—if we were, people would question our emotional stability. Others have narrowly defined our expected emotional reactions, and by and large, all of us follow the script. We almost never create an emotional state preemptive to a situation. We just go around reacting and reacting. It's a kind of devastating idea, isn't it?

Now imagine for a moment that we turn this idea on its head: Instead of waiting for other people and situations to determine how we feel, we feel the emotion we want to feel first, then allow the people and situations to come into our lives to support these feelings. This means that when we wake up in the morning, we anticipate having a wonderful, fantastic day. We sense the emotions of wonder and anticipation bubbling through us that something really good is going to occur, and we've created an emotional state out of nothing. There's no event that we're reacting to; rather, we're allowing the events of the day to react to *us*.

There's a good chance that if you try this experiment, it will be the first time in your life that you've chosen an emotional state before it has chosen you. It can feel odd at first to summon up an emotional state without a corresponding "reason" to have it, but the results can be bizarrely spectacular as events start reacting to *you*.

As the day progresses, one thing you'll notice is how difficult it becomes to maintain this reversal—it's as if the wave of conditioning we're all so used to is crushingly thick. At some point, you'll once again begin to become *re*active rather than *pro*active, often without your even noticing.

However, Flowdreaming is a great place to start practicing gaining control over the emotional habit. The idea in Track 2 of the CD is to learn to consciously evoke an emotional state. The emotional state you invoke in the Flow becomes the pattern for the emotions that you want to see more of in your life. Whatever feelings you experience in the Flow come back to you in the rest of your life, in greater measure, as situations are created to support these feelings. Your life doesn't want to create a mismatch, so you program the Flow with the emotions you want, and your reality tends to shape itself to match.

In this exercise, you're asked to create a feeling of happiness and acceptance inside your body. You can feel it wherever you sense the seat of your emotions as being. Interestingly, most people don't sense this seat as being in their head or brain—rather, they feel it in their guts or stomach area, and often in the heart or chest. As you experiment, you'll find your own seat, and from it, you'll sense the emotion building up there. You can feel it energetically as a bubbling, rising, engulfing sensation that spreads through and out of you.

It may help to remember a time when you felt an overwhelming good feeling before. Perhaps the first time you held your baby, you had an overwhelming feeling of unconditional love. Maybe during a loved one's illness, you experienced an engulfing feeling of forgiveness and gratitude. Harken back to those feelings to get a sense of the completeness of the feeling you're creating. By purposefully creating an emotional feeling in the Flow, you create a pattern (or template) for more of this feeling to come into your life. So if you're sensing, for instance, that an abundance of money is heading your way, you're both creating the event (money heading to you) as well as your emotional experience of it (joy, acceptance, total good feelings about its source and its place in your life). The emotion is what goes out and "grabs" this event for you—it's what makes your daydream more than just fancy images flitting through your head. It's the anchor that embeds the desire into the Flow.

It's important that you practice this exercise as much as you need to in order to get really good at bringing your emotional energy into the Flow, and before we go on to the next step in the process.

CHAPTER FOUR

Flowdreaming Step-by-Step

So how exactly *do* you Flowdream? Well, once you listen to Tracks 4 through 6 on the CD, you should have a pretty good idea of what the process feels like. Still, here are the basics written out to guide you. Remember that Flowdreaming is easy, natural, and instinctual. It's also *individual,* so what works for me or someone else might need modifying for you. Consider the steps that follow as guidelines.

1. Start by closing your eyes and relaxing. Take a few deep breaths and relax the areas of your body where you hold tension, especially your stomach, shoulders, neck, jaw, and forehead. Taking a few moments to unwind should help you go deeper into your daydreaming, so you'll experience a fuller, more profound Flow.

2. Remind yourself that, in essence, you're just daydreaming. You already know how to do this, so it's going to be easy for you—there are no criteria for doing it "right."

3. Create some imagery that leads you into the flowing river of energy that is the Flow. You may see an arc of energy through the air that you mentally follow until you land in the rushing Flow energy. Perhaps you'll sense a door that you open and walk through to reach this place. Or you might start by immediately pretending that you're bouncing along in a rolling river of energy and feeling the current surrounding your physical body, which sways with the current. Some people find that slightly moving and swaying their body, as if they were gently floating downriver on a boat, makes it easier to conjure up the flow in their minds. Try a variety of techniques to find the one that suits you best.

My favorite way to begin is to feel my body as being nothing but energy—that is, I mentally dissolve the physical part of myself and sense instead the swirling mass of energy that creates my body. Then I think of the air and the objects that surround me as nothing but energy, too—they've just been stamped into different patterns, like the same cookie dough cut into varying shapes to bake.

Once I sense this underlying energy in both myself and the things surrounding me, I then note that all of this moves in a particular direction, and I allow my body to "lock in" to it, much like the jarring feeling of a roller-coaster car locking on to its track. Sometimes I even feel a little "snapping" sensation as my body locks in to the Flow. This is all very kinesthetic—I really use my physical body to feel this occurring. Sometime during this locking-in process, I begin to see the Flow surrounding me as coursing waves of sparkling light. I sense that it's the energetic underpinning of all I see around me; it's where the individual Flow of all objects and thoughts around me meet and mingle to create the world I experience.

It's right around this point that I make a natural transition from really concentrating into a more relaxed, effortless daydreaming state. On days when I'm stressed, it takes a little longer to make the transition, and I find myself working harder to see and sense these initial images; on days when I'm relaxed and feeling positive, however, the shift occurs much faster.

4. Once you're in the Flow, make it look whatever way you want. It can appear like flowing cosmic energy; a web of translucent strings of light; a warm, bubbling, crystalline stream; a smooth, gliding road; or whatever works for you. Feel it around you, and sense the pace with which it carries you. If it seems as if you're shooting down a luge track, you might want to slow it down; on the other hand, if you're barely moving at all, speed up a bit by adding some current to your Flow. Pay attention to what the speed might be communicating to you about the velocity of your life.

Likewise, you may find yourself moving straight ahead; or you may feel as if you're stuck in a side pool, meandering, or otherwise not going forward. Use these feelings as status reports from the Greater You about the current Flow of your life. You may indeed be stuck in a stagnant side pool—if this is the case, gently imagine yourself swimming back into the flowing center.

5. Think aloud in your mind as you guide yourself down the river of your Flow. Or try not to concentrate on words at all, but allow your mind to shift imagery at will, just like when you normally daydream. Within this "energy river," evoke the feeling of whatever it is you want to attract in your life. How does it feel to have this? Go for the intended feeling you'll get from the object or experience rather than focusing on the thing itself. You'll find that as you start imagining the things you want to manifest, your mind will drift away from the Flow imagery and summon instead the imagery and emotions surrounding what you're creating in your future.

6. Remember to use all five senses. Smell the grass if you're envisioning nature, and feel the texture of $100 bills in your hands if you're visualizing money. And use any of the common images on the CD, such as seeing your body as a magnet if you're trying to attract something.

7. Be sure to feel lots of positive emotion around whatever it is you're imagining. Stay purposeful as you create whatever feelings and emotions you want to experience in your life. What you create in the Flow state is what you're directing yourself to bring into your life. Having a sense

of thankfulness declares that your desire has already come true. Feeling overwhelming joy expresses that the very best of events have occurred for you, leaving you in a profound state of happiness at the result. This is a critical point for you to understand: You're "pre-experiencing" the emotions you want to have in your life, so whatever you choose to feel is what you're bringing in to yourself.

Think of it as imprinting the energy field with the emotions you wish to have more of in your life. If you send out the emotions of gratitude and satisfaction, for instance, then you'll be creating an underlying energy pattern that will bring into existence situations where you feel gratitude and satisfaction in all areas of your life. I can't stress enough that *whatever feelings you imprint the Flow energy with are the same feelings that will come back to you in your everyday life*. The situations that surround you will support these emotions, so if you feel joy, then situations will come to you that evoke joy. If you feel relief, then things will happen around you that make you feel relieved. If you feel love, then you'll increasingly find yourself feeling love in all areas of your life: "I love this new job that came to me!" "I love the new house I found," "I love the intimacy my daughter and I are now experiencing," and so on.

Remember: *Your emotions are much more powerful attractors than any images you invoke.* Even if you don't see anything at all, if the emotional energy you generate could fill a football field, then you're still in fine shape!

8. Envision whatever general outcomes you want to occur in your life. (See the beginning of Chapter 5 for more about general versus specific desires.) Again, your intention is to *imprint* or *repattern* the Flow energy with whatever you're seeing and feeling. You're creating an energetic blueprint that will then direct your Flow and the Flows of all the tools and materials involved in your desire.

9. Remind yourself that your being in the Flow will continue even after your Flowdream ends and you open your eyes. Tell yourself that you've now "corrected course" and repatterned the energy, and your life will reflect the adjustments you just made.

10. End your Flowdream by again going into the flowing river of energy.

There's no litmus test for being in the Flow, or performing this process correctly. If you feel lots of energy or surges of strong emotion around the images you see and thoughts you have, if you can successfully "see" the stream of energy or water, or if you can feel the energy around your body extending out into the atmosphere around you, then you're Flowdreaming.

A Plan for Getting Started

The beauty of Flowdreaming is that it's an incredibly flexible process—you can do it anytime, anywhere. But if you want to get started with some structure, here's a suggested schedule to help you get comfortable with the process.

First, choose a time to set aside every day. For the first week, allow yourself 15 minutes each day . . . this could be after your morning grooming but before you start the rest of the activities of your day, as you sit in your car (not while it's running!) before you begin the drive to work, the first 15 minutes of your lunch break, or in the tub in the evening. These are all points when you normally rest your mind, since they come before or after other activities. Your mind is already used to "winding down" or transitioning during these periods, so they make natural places to start.

Note that you should try to avoid winding-down periods that occur late at night, such as when you're watching the 11 o'clock news on TV. By this time, your mind is already tired from the day, and it's harder to summon that emotional energy you'll need.

For the first week or two, begin by using the enclosed CD and alternate playing either preliminary exercise (Track 2 or 3) right before you play Track 4 ("Flowdreaming for the Best of Everything"). The first two tracks will strengthen your skills, while Track 4 seeks to course correct any out-of-balance situations in your life. I really do urge you to play Track 4 regularly—it's the best Flowdream for tackling any and all situations in life to bring about the best future possible.

After you've used these three tracks for a while, you may wish to move on to the other Flowdreams on the CD. (You can also go to the Website at **www.flowdreaming. com** to learn about other CDs that focus on specific areas of your life, such as attracting a romantic relationship, improving your health, repairing your body after surgery, building a business, gaining advancement in your career, creating a luxurious lifestyle for yourself, releasing depression, and more.)

If you have a specific situation that you'd like to address in your life, create a Flowdream of your own using some of the guidelines presented in this chapter. Re-create this Flowdream daily until you start noticing a shift in events in your life. (See "How to Know If Flowdreaming Is Working" on page 71.)

If you're still wondering exactly how much time each day to devote to Flowdreaming, keep this in mind: Most people, including myself, find it difficult to sustain the kind of imagery and heightened emotion required in Flowdreaming for more than 10 to 20 minutes at a time, so Flowdreaming is usually self-limiting. You can, however, Flowdream as often as you want: once a day, twice a day, and so on. You don't always need to spend 15 minutes at it, either—maybe you just want to spend 5 minutes every few hours realigning yourself with your own positive Flow throughout the day. Just close your eyes and do it!

Design a program that's easy enough for you to stick with. Maybe you can only muster up five minutes a day, every few days. If so, don't worry—it's better than nothing, and way more than you were doing before you picked up this book, when you didn't Flowdream at all.

I Flowdream almost every evening for about 10 to 15 minutes. And I often do it sporadically during the day, when I sense that a situation around me isn't going the way I want. I get into the Flow and try to release my expectations about the situation (in case I've started to unknowingly "swim upstream"), and I feel myself flowing toward the greatest good in my life and allowing the situation I'm encountering to fall into alignment with my desire.

Useful Flowdream Images and Sensations

As you continue your Flowdreaming, you may discover certain recurring images or sensations that hold special power or meaning for you. By all means, develop and use them frequently. Some of the most useful include:

- Seeing and feeling your body as a giant magnet, pulling whatever it is you want toward you

- A feeling of reaching into the sky or air

- Flowing in a stream or river of water or energy

- Sensing the molecules of your body and the molecules of the air around you as mixing freely together, erasing the boundaries between them

- A pool or fountain of energy that contains whatever you're manifesting

- Feeling as if the thing you're manifesting has already occurred, and you're reacting to it emotionally with happiness, thankfulness, and awe

- Feeling whatever it is you're manifesting as covering you, like a blanket, or that it has become a part of you and you and it are mingling together

- Seeing other people as part of your Flow, helping you and facilitating your requests

- Feeling strongly that you expect good luck and perfect timing to start manifesting in your life

This list will continue to grow as you Flowdream and stumble on emotions and images that work for you.

Now that you've got the basics of this process down, let's learn how to Flowdream in the most effective way we can.

CHAPTER FIVE

Getting What You Want in the Flow

At its heart, Flowdreaming is an intense method of manifesting. It's repatterning the energy around you so that your Flow *and* the individual Flows of all the things around you come together to lay the blueprint for whatever it is you want to manifest.

Now this next idea is very important: *The most effective Flowdream that creates the absolute most beneficial outcome for you is one that allows for the broadest number of good things to come to you, with no restrictions.* In other words, shed the specifics and just feel enormous bounty, goodwill, luck, joyful synchronicity, and general positivity in your life by affirming: "Everything is happening at the right time and the right place in my life, and I'm open to receiving all that that entails."

Why should this affirmation be so general? Well, as an exercise, spend a few moments thinking about each specific thing you wish for as a *restriction*. For instance, maybe you really want a new Volkswagen Beetle. You go in the Flow and *feel* that car coming to you with every fiber of your being, to the point that you even see yourself at the dealership purchasing it.

But what's happening here is that by concentrating on this particular vehicle at the dealership, you're closing off access to other modes of getting it. In other words, you're placing restrictions around the car that limit the opportunities the Universe may bring you for accepting it. Perhaps that same Beetle can be obtained for a better price elsewhere, yet you've closed off that avenue by focusing on the dealership. So the best thing to do is expand your desire a little bit and focus just on the car, not the dealership.

At the same time, maybe you're going into the Flow to find a better career. What happens if the career and car don't intersect favorably? Perhaps your best career is, unexpectedly, one that takes you overseas for a while. Then what will you do with this brand-new car? You'll have to either sell it at a loss or pay for storage . . . so maybe this new vehicle isn't the best thing for you after all.

Instead, what if you imagined a perfect means of transportation for yourself while at the same time focusing on the perfect career opportunity that could come your way? You might find yourself driving the brand-new Beetle of a friend who isn't currently using it, while at the same time, the perfect overseas job arises. Now these two different desires have found the perfect "pattern" to allow both in your life, but chances are that you couldn't have envisioned this particular confluence of events yourself. You left it up to the Flow to mastermind it—you just did the asking.

This is an extreme example, but do you see how opening up from the detailed to the general expands the avenue of opportunity for the best things to come to you? At the most extreme end, perhaps you let go of the car *and* the job, and you go into the Flow and feel yourself being an incredibly happy person whose every need is filled. Perhaps you add that you have extraordinarily fulfilling work each day with the best possible transportation. And you live rather comfortably in an area that's harmonious with your nature, with enough wealth to support your lifestyle. Finally, you envision supportive, wonderful friendships and a loving family.

This now takes every restriction off the possibilities that can come to you because you've opened up to the general in each account, with the only condition being that whatever comes to you brings you absolute joy. You have no worries because you know that whatever you get will be something you're extremely happy with.

Of course this kind of Flowdream isn't going to be satisfying enough for most of us, because we've become attached to "things." We already have a vision of what will make us most happy, and we think we know best. Never mind that as we look back, we can see a constant pattern of wanting something we think will make us happy, then getting it and moving on to the next thing we want, creating a continuous cycle of never being quite satisfied enough. Our pasts are littered with these fulfilled and unfulfilled wants, but at the moment, we still want *more*. It's difficult to break away from this cycle, and the strong materialistic focus of our society just keeps on feeding it.

So one exercise is to instead open up to allowing the *best things* to come to you, period, for one month. Imagine long-lasting happiness, love, and harmony in your emotional life, and feelings of contentment and satisfaction with your work, home, and finances. And let come what comes, as long as it fits in with these very broad desires.

This allows for new, complex patterns to arise in your life that you probably wouldn't think of yourself. Your life is a mishmash of one thing depending on or supporting another. Your home is dependent on your paycheck, your paycheck is dependent on your job, your job is dependent on your skills, and so on. If one link in this chain of dependencies (or these "patterns of interactions") is disrupted, the entire chain will fall apart.

Centering your life around the Flow, however, seeks an organizing principle much greater than yourself. It places the burden of finding the "best possible" and "most right" outcomes into a higher patterning principle, and removes it from your own lesser mind. Straight Flow is when you access this greater organizing principle, sync yourself up with it, and say, "Go for it—bring me the best things for me. Put me in harmony with the greatest good for myself and others."

This is why at the beginning and ending of every Flowdream, you go into the flowing stream of water or universal energy and feel yourself relaxing into the positive direction—straight Flow. This is like gold, because even if you concentrate on those other, specific things you want, you're still opening enough into your Flow to allow them to come to you *only* if they fit into the higher patterns of your life. You're basically saying, "Here's what I want. Bring it to me if it fits; if it doesn't, bring me something better."

Consequently, you're taken out of the position of being the cop directing traffic in the busy intersection of your life. If you allocate that to the Flow, you can instead spend your time experiencing the richness of what comes to you. Interestingly, this philosophy finds similar tenets within many religions. "Let go and let God" is a popular saying that finds close similarity to "Let go into the Flow."

How to Tell If You're in the Flow

Some days while you Flowdream, you'll find that no matter what you do, you're distracted, listening to every noise in your environment, worrying about little issues that suddenly arise, and so forth. If this happens to you, then just mentally shrug your shoulders and allow yourself to drift into whatever depth of Flow you can achieve that day. There will always be other days and more opportunities to go into your Flow. There's never a good reason to feel that you have to get it right every time; if you feel that way often, you're putting too much pressure on yourself and should spend some time thinking about your ideas of perfection and/or achievement.

Most of the time, however, you'll find yourself drifting into an "average" state of Flow. This so-called average depth is unique to you, and you'll begin to recognize it after you've been going in the Flow for a while. Gradually, you'll be able to go in faster and deeper according to the natural progression of your body. Don't hurry things—allow your mind to develop at its own speed. There is no "should" depth to attain. The following guidelines, however, will let you evaluate the degree of Flow you'll ultimately want to experience.

1. During the guided Flowdream, you lose track of time.

2. You sense vibrations, heaviness, fluttering, or quivering in your body; a gathered surge of energy at a particular location in your body; or a feeling of tickling, caressing, or the hairs rising on your skin during the Flow.

3. You see one or more of your Flow images with incredible clarity.

4. You experience long or short bursts of strong emotion.

5. At any time, you sense a sudden overwhelming union or interconnection with whatever you're imagining (this might feel as if your body has merged with your vision or imagined outcome). You'll want to hold on to this feeling of union whenever it occurs.

6. You feel an overwhelming sense of certainty surrounding something that you're imagining.

7. Images, words, emotions, or other sensations come to you—almost as if from another (positive) source—communicating something that you feel sure you didn't think of yourself. This might be a message about a situation, a vision of something, or a sudden understanding—but mainly it feels as if someone were trying to convey something to you, and you just unexpectedly received the information.

If this happens, consider yourself lucky, as the Greater You is passing yourself a message. Accept it; if it's unclear, ask your Flow to show you what it means. Don't be afraid to ask again and again to make the message clearer to you. It isn't a puzzle to solve—you have every interest in obtaining the clearest communication possible.

8. You experience premonitions. Remember that the Flow is outside of time, so you're in a state where the future and the present are mingled. If you see something that feels future oriented, accept it gratefully and overwhelm it with positive feelings. (I regularly receive extremely short-term premonitions—for things as near as a day ahead.)

9. You have a sense of being able to "feel" the air around you, almost like a viscous fluid or gel, and you have a sense of interacting with it.

10. You experience waking REM (rapid eye movement). This feels as if your eyelids are rapidly fluttering, without any effort on your part to cause it.

It might be helpful to think of going in the Flow as being like traveling on a wet dirt road in a car: The first few times you roll by, the wheels make only slight impressions in the earth—that is, they don't sink in much. But over time, as the car keeps going over the same route, the wheels sink deeper and deeper, creating significant grooves. As you go over and over the same path in the Flow, you'll also find yourself going deeper as your mind becomes accustomed to the route. You will truly have gotten "in the groove."

How to Know If Flowdreaming Is Working

After a while, you may start to wonder if the process is actually working for you. A way to tell is by noticing any unusual opportunities that may have come up in your life since you started Flowdreaming. They may or may not relate to exactly the thing you're trying to manifest, but pay attention anyway. One thing has a way of leading to another, because Flowdreaming is ultimately about changing the *patterns* in your life.

For example, think back on all the steps you took to get to the job or career you have now. You can see some pivotal moments where you know that if you'd made a single different decision, you wouldn't be where you are now. Perhaps you received a phone call from an old friend, who then later introduced you to his sister, who mentioned that the company where she works was looking for someone with your qualifications . . . and shortly after that, you landed the job.

Hearing from your friend was in and of itself only slightly unusual, but since it coincided with a point in your life when you were looking for job and his sister's company was hiring, you effectively followed a flow or pattern of events that led to where you are now. In other words, it was so easy that you almost felt that it was a "set-up" event in your life. I'm sure that you've experienced this kind of curious chain of events somewhere in your life, which can show you whether you're *in* or *out* of the Flow.

Speaking of being out of the Flow, some days when I go out on errands, I find that the home-improvement store doesn't have the kind of lightbulb I'm looking for, the drive-through car wash at the gas station is temporarily closed even though I just bought the ticket, the dry cleaning that was supposed to be ready isn't, the grocery store is out of the diapers I want to buy, I drive endlessly around parking lots looking for a place to park while the guy in back of me always seems to get a spot that opens up just as I move up the row, and so on. Nothing is going my way—it's almost as if the morning was cursed and I should have just stayed home.

But rather than cursed, I choose to see the morning as just being out of the Flow. When this kind of thing happens, I wonder if I haven't gotten stuck in a bad "current," and somehow I need to break the connection. Stopping what I'm doing, retreating, and going about those same errands later has always helped. In other words, the best way to break any negative trend is to simply stop and change direction.

Now, as you look for indications that you're *in* the Flow, you need to note these chains of events where instead of everything going wrong, things just fall into place for you naturally, one after another. This "falling-into place" is what you're ultimately concentrating on when you're in the Flow, along with feelings of ease or being in the right place at the right time, finding unexpected opportunities, and having things "go your way." You should look for these characteristics in whatever situation you're focusing on. In some cases, you'll only see these qualities in retrospect, such as in the example about the career, but if you're consciously watching, you can often see the chain of events as it occurs.

If you find yourself being blocked during this process, take it as a sign that you're swimming upstream where the current is against you. You might want to step back and reassess the choices you're making—for example, maybe you can get to the same goal through a different route. Finding yourself blocked or thwarted and seeing problems around every corner is a sign that the choices you're making aren't in your best interests. This doesn't mean, however, that you need to completely abandon your goals, or that your goals themselves aren't in your best interests—perhaps they are, perhaps they aren't . . . only time will tell.

Instead, go into the Flow and envision that the right way to go about things is made clear to you, and that opportunities for the best way to accomplish your desires come to you. Reroute the energy into the best channel—if you continue to be thwarted, consider broadening your desires to ask that the *best* things come to you in your situation, letting go of the "particulars." Perhaps there's something even better for you out there, but as long as you tie yourself to the person or situation you *think* is best, true happiness will remain elusive.

Follow Your Hunches

One of the major ideas of the Flow is that you're making things easier for yourself. This is a tricky point, because "easy" doesn't mean "lazy." Being in the Flow doesn't mean that you simply sit back and wait for stuff to happen to you or watch opportunities pass by when they come because you're too lazy to make a move. Remember that "doing nothing" is as much of a choice as choosing to do *something.* Action and inaction are both, in a sense, actions.

Instead, being in the Flow means deliberately looking for and choosing actions and situations that feel most in harmony with your being—that's what is meant by "ease." This translates into practicality as you: (1) put out your requests into the Flow; (2) look for the results of your requests as they manifest in your life; and (3) take action on those results.

So again, the key idea is to *choose actions and situations that feel most in harmony with your being.* The Flow will increase the frequency of these actions and situations in your life, but you still have to recognize and act on them. Sometimes the results of your Flowdreaming will be obvious, such as when you wish for a new relationship and get one. At other times, you'll find yourself following your feelings or hunches.

We're all guided by myriad conscious and subconscious information, as well as an intuitive sense. When you choose a checkout line in the supermarket, for instance, you probably scan all the other lines to assess which one will be fastest. But you don't stop and consciously tick off a list of all the criteria you're assessing—rather, you gather your information so quickly that you don't even tend to realize that you're doing it. Ultimately, you put yourself in a line and follow your hunch, picking the one that "feels" right. However, if you use your mind to rationally assess the different lengths and base your decision on how many shopping carts are ahead of you, bypassing your intuition, you can often get caught waiting the longest when the only person in front of you starts disputing the bill and a manager is called in to check prices . . . you know the drill.

Following your hunches means asking, "Does the situation feel right? Does it feel within my Flow?" Here's another example of what "feeling the energy of situation" is like: Have you ever noticed how on the mornings of national holidays, such as Thanksgiving or Christmas, the world feels calmer and more serene? When you step outside on these mornings, there's a palpable sense of serenity almost in the air itself. The only reason I can think for this happening is that a national holiday is one of the few times when almost everyone has the day off work. Shops are closed, people are feeling less stressed, and many people are relaxing—the constant national mental chatter is turned *off*. The normal activity of millions of people is momentarily quieted, and it's as if our national Flow makes a remarkable shift from noisy hubbub to inward quietude.

Next holiday, go stand outside for a moment in the morning and soak in this feeling. Let it be a reminder of how your intuitive sense is attuned to the world round you. Follow your hunches, for they'll lead you to your Flow.

CHAPTER SIX

Flowdreaming
Questions and Answers

The following are some of the most common questions that people have asked me about Flowdreaming. I hope the answers will help you as well.

Q. Can I bring other people into the Flow with me? Would they have to know about it?

A. Sometimes the things you want in life involve another person: Maybe you want a hot romance with someone in particular; you need a raise at work but aren't sure if your boss will go for the idea; or someone you love is ill, and you want them to find the best treatment. It's possible in any of these situations to simply take the person into the Flow with you. And no, they don't need to be present or even know what you're doing.

Begin Flowdreaming the way that you usually do. When you find yourself completely in your Flow, sensing the waves of energy or the positive flow of the current, "look" or feel around in your mind until you spot the person you want to Flow with you. Sense them riding the current, too. You can use whatever imagery you want for bringing other people into the Flow: Visualize them on a pool float, skateboard, or surfboard; see them in a rowboat; or feel them holding your hand as you skim the Flow together. Use whatever imagery works for you.

Next, sense waves of emotion, both for what you want in particular to have happen as well as for the absolute best thing for both of you. This latter part is particularly important. You see, you can broadcast what you want to have happen, but you must keep in mind that what you want may not be in the best interests of the other person. So you need to keep an open mind for a solution that works for *both* of you. It's likely that it will be something you don't currently have enough information to imagine, so feeling the "best" solution is the right thing to do.

As an example, several years ago my grandmother was diagnosed with lung cancer. My mother and I both went into the Flow together and felt my grandmother's illness dissolving away. Then we imagined all three of us in the Flow. In my mind, I saw myself, my mom, and my grandmother in a warm stream of thick, sparkling energy that was gently carrying us all in the most positive, joy-filled direction. And I felt moments of intense anticipation as I encountered unexpected good things coming to us. It didn't matter that I didn't see the specifics of what those things were—I just felt the emotion that I'd experience in real life if something perfect and healing came our way.

Throughout the process, my mother kept a running commentary of what she was seeing so that I could follow along (much in the same way that you'll follow my voice on the enclosed CD). Mom decided that rather than imagining her mother just flowing with us in the stream, she should be carried in a glimmering chariot. So we both saw my grandmother resting easily in this chariot, which we helped float forward in the Flow. We imagined that anything in her life that was contributing to her ill health or unhappiness was drifting away behind her—since it was no longer useful, she could therefore discard it. We felt the right treatment come to her and saw her as radiantly healthy.

We later repeated this same Flowdream with the participation of eight other members of our family. We all sat in a circle, and my mother and I took turns guiding us all. (When you Flowdream with more that one person, you'll find the intensity of the Flowdream greatly enhanced.)

Now it happens that when my grandmother was first diagnosed, her doctor had told her that she was too old to withstand the difficult surgery she'd need, so instead she should accept the cancer and make the most of her remaining months. She went to another doctor, who told her that he'd be willing to perform the surgery, but because they'd be sawing open her ribs, she'd have to live in a nursing home for three to six months, with very little activity, while she healed. She'd be enormously weakened by such a long stay, and there was no guarantee that she then wouldn't become a permanent member of that rest home. She scheduled the surgery anyway.

After putting my grandmother in the Flow twice, however, a new solution arose within a week. My aunt encountered a woman who knew someone who had just undergone a little-known kind of treatment for tumors that didn't involve surgery. It relied on proton lasers to selectively target the cancer, so no cutting was involved. After getting more information, the doctors at this new clinic told my grandmother that she was a perfect candidate, so she scheduled this treatment instead of surgery. Today, she's cancer free.

So you see, by continuing to ask for the best possible solution in the Flow, my family encountered successively better treatment options, until the final one involving proton therapy—the one that felt most right—came to us.

Months later, after a number of tests came back showing complete remission, my grandmother visited a local doctor because she had a chest cold. He looked at her medical chart and promptly asked her why she was still alive. "You had an aggressive carcinoma," he said. "You should be dead!" What he meant to impart was that she should be very happy to be alive, and a cold was the least of her worries. What he inadvertently communicated, however, was something that none of her other physicians had revealed—that her particular kind of cancer was usually deadly, with or without treatment. Doctors know, by and large, that the ideas they put into a patient's head inevitably affect the treatment outcome. Each of my grandmother's doctors instinctively withheld this information from her, and the result was that she always expected to be cured . . . and she was.

Coincidence? Perhaps. But that is what the Flow is all about—coincidence, synchronicity, and increasing your odds of being in the right place at the right time as perfect solutions come to you.

Q. How do I know that I'm not changing other people's destinies if I picture them in the Flow?

A. As long as you always ask for the best for others, you're only helping them have more experiences that will allow them to act from their own highest state of being. I recently heard from a woman who had remarried, and her little daughter now had a stepfather. He was loving and kind, and the girl felt that he was her new father figure. But the girl's biological father was hurt and jealous because he felt replaced. A struggle between the two men ensued: Who would be her "real" father? Could she call them both "Daddy"? The fight between the two men had escalated, and the little girl felt confused and wrong—an outcome neither "father" would ever wish on his daughter. The mother asked, "How can I use the Flow to figure out who my daughter's father should really be?"

The first thing we did was rephrase the question. "Let's go in the Flow," I advised, "and instead affirm: 'I feel that both men place their own egos aside and are given opportunities to act in the best interests of my daughter. I see them both stepping up to the plate and allowing their best fatherly instincts to pour from them, giving only love and immediately sensing in their own hearts what is best for my daughter. I see my daughter smiling and filled with love for them. I sense an exchange all around that creates the best possible solution that pleases everyone. We are all so happy and filled with delight because the solution has already come into being. I accept it into our lives.'"

By doing this, the woman and I took the pressure off of her to think up the best solution—instead, we left that chore to the infinite possibilities that exist in the Flow. Rather than drawing from the woman's own limited pool of answers, we opened it up to assess everyone's part and draw from an infinite number of solutions. Each man involved was now given the opportunity to feel a loving interest in living up to his own fatherly potential, and in no way did this harm or misdirect either one of them. As you can see, the Flow will offer a solution that allows everyone to feel satisfied.

You should never sense that something is too good to be true. The moment you feel that, you've closed off an avenue for yourself. And as long as you ask that anyone else you involve in your Flow be treated in the best possible way, you're likewise affirming that you'll be treated just the same. A good rule of thumb is this: *Whatever energy you put out in the Flow, whether for yourself or someone else, will infuse the energy surrounding your own self.* So hate, anger, and retribution all close doors in the Flow, while at the same time increasing those feelings all throughout your own life. It's an energetic inevitability. (This is also just another way of reiterating the Golden Rule.)

Q. What if I feel negative emotions in the Flow, such as worry or anxiety?

A. Getting a grip on emotions in the Flow can be the most challenging part for some people, especially if they feel at some level that it's irrational to feel things without a reason for them. Instead of staying with the positive, joyful emotions they go in with, their minds slip into habit mode and they "wake up" in the middle of the Flowdream to find themselves fretting about something. And then they panic: *Oh no, now I'm going to get more anxiety and worry in my life since I just felt that in the Flow!*

No worries here—remember that it's the *process* that truly counts. If you in fact find yourself inadvertently worrying over a situation in the Flow, all you need to do is see the solution coming into place. You can just notice the negative emotion and then sense it leaving you, floating free from you in the warm, sparkling energy. You might even see it seeping out and away from you like a gray haze as you speed forward away from it—sense it leaving, gone forever.

You've just acknowledged a negative emotional state and created the remedy for it all in one step, and you've further created a new pattern of releasing in the Flow that will carry through into your daily life. That is, you've planted the energetic seed for *releasing* the emotion.

You can also affirm: "The situation that caused that concern has already been fixed. A solution has already been found, and I allow this solution to come easily and quickly into my life. I see the solution right here, right now, and I feel utter thankfulness for it. My prayers have been answered."

Incidentally, the assertion "My prayers have been answered" is one of the most powerful phrases you can utter in the Flow. Use it regularly.

Q. What if nothing happens and I don't see anything?

A. Rarely, people close their eyes, listen to the CD, and see . . . nothing. This lack of imagery is disappointing, and their anxiety or agitation only feeds the problem, creating more nothing. In this case, the individuals are usually working with a preconceived set of ideas that's blocking them from the experience. This includes thinking that these images are supposed to come from somewhere outside of them to be communicated *to* them, so they wait like receivers for something to come. Often, images do tend to feel as if they're being given to you from an outside, intelligent force, but when Flowdreaming, *you* are the one who creates and directs all the initial imagery and sensation. Anything that comes to you from the "outside" is a bonus.

Other people go into the Flow, sense the river, and then lose focus. Their minds wander and they move into a nondirected daydream. All that's occurred is that they failed to maintain conscious control over that daydream. They should just repeat the process until they start to stay with it longer and longer. (Again, this is rarely a problem for most people.)

People who are visually impaired can Flowdream as easily as anyone else. Instead of "seeing" the Flow in their mind, they can just use the other senses they normally use as they explore the Flow.

And finally, for anyone who just feels out of practice with daydreaming, remember that *you* are the one in charge here, so you create the images and initiate the scenes. In other words, you can just make something up—it's not "cheating" to do so. If your imagination is sluggish, then use imagery from popular movies to get you started. Use scenes of interstellar wormholes or matrixes or anything you've seen on the big screen. Your own imagination will take over at some point.

Q. Flowdreaming seems good for changing the future, but can I alter the past, too?

A. We've been talking a lot about how Flowdreaming can affect your future as you use it to manifest what you want in your life. But what about your past? Since you're truly accessing the Universal Mind—where everything that is, was, or will be is existing in an extraordinarily rich environment of frothing cosmic possibilities—then shouldn't the past be as accessible as the future?

Absolutely. Now I'm not suggesting that you can go back in time and physically relive your past. But you can hop in the Flow and *mentally* change any situation you can remember. Even though changing events on a physical level may be closed off to you, changing events at the *energetic* level is still an option. Most of us have never tried this before because we've never been taught that we could do it, let alone how. But speak to any physicist today, even the eminent Stephen Hawking, and he'll tell you that time travel must exist, because nothing in the laws of physics prevents it . . . he just can't tell you how it could be done. Perhaps someday, accessing the past through an expanded level of consciousness could hold a key to unraveling the mystery of realistic time travel.

Nonetheless, the point of changing past events today at an energetic level is to create a second probable outcome where only one had existed before. In your Flow, you're in essence "switching" from one outcome (the physical situation that happened in your past, which you've accepted) to a new one that you create today in the Flow. If all your subsequent choices and opportunities came from your original physically experienced situation, then can you see how, by changing the energetic effects of that situation, you're allowing new choices and opportunities to come to you?

As an example, let me tell you how I first discovered this. One day while Flowdreaming, a memory from grade school of something that had actually occurred suddenly popped into my mind: A boy whom I had a crush on had finally noticed me and had walked up to me and asked if he could help me carry the heavy science-fair project I was struggling with. I was so shy that I told him I could carry it by myself. He asked again, then left. He never tried to help me or showed interest in me again, and I imagine that his asking meant getting over his own incredible shyness. My rebuff was enough to scare him away for good.

For years, I'd scolded myself about what a dummy I'd been. The memory stuck with me because I secretly wondered if it was really childhood shyness, or was it just one of the first expressions of a debilitating need for self-sufficiency that was preventing me from accepting help from others in my life today? Since I was deeply in the Flow, I brought this little boy's image to mind and replayed the entire scene. But this time I accepted his help, and we joked and talked all the way to my mother's car, where we stored the project he'd carried for me.

More than just seeing this, I *felt* it. I experienced my initial shyness (and his), and then I felt how easily we talked together and laughed, and how we decided to be friends. I felt these emotions move through my body, and I was even actually smiling in my chair as I was seeing all this in the Flow. Most of all, I felt that *this* was the real way it had happened, so I let go of the other way—I felt my attachment to it releasing right out of my stomach area, which I sensed was where I was holding it.

When I came out of the Flow, I felt that I'd actually made a significant change. I haven't ever worried about that day again, because I know that I'd energetically corrected the situation. Remember that your Flow, as an energetic manifestation of your consciousness existing both in *and* outside of time and space, stores everything you've experienced. Rewriting the data—essentially adding to that data—is a completely valid form of changing your Flow.

Q. I already meditate—how is Flowdreaming different? And can I do them together?

A. The varieties of meditation in the world today are myriad. Many have evolved into formalized art forms, such as the Zen technique, or they're based on specialized meditation tools such as pranic yogi breathing and formalized mantras. These practices can take years to perfect.

But no matter what the form, most types of meditation have core similarities, such as the central tenet of stilling or quieting the mind. To achieve this, those meditating learn to focus on their breathing or on a single image in the mind, or they use sounds such as "oommm" or "ahhhh" or chanting to keep their attention centered. The goal has been to prevent the mind from straying into all kinds of jibber-jabber ("Am I doing it? Oh darn, my mind was quiet for a second, then I asked myself if I was keeping quiet, and that broke the silence. How many more minutes do I have left with this? Do I have to add on time because I keep talking to myself? Okay, I'm being quiet again. *[Silence]* Wow, how long was that?! Oh, only 30 seconds," and so on)

Once the mental chatter ceases, a person will find him- or herself experiencing alpha brain waves, which act as a bridge between the conscious and subconscious mind. Alpha waves are associated with visualization and daydreaming, and past biofeedback research has shown that a person can increase the number of alpha waves they produce by relaxing and experiencing guided imagery. And deeper meditation evokes theta brain waves, which represent access to the subconscious mind, as well to stores of creativity, memory, emotion, and feeling or sensation.

Similar to traditional meditation, getting in the Flow means altering your mental state to tap these deeper levels of brain waves. In fact, recent studies have shown that daydreaming can bring your mind into the same theta-wave state as meditation.

However, unlike traditional meditation, which focuses on stilling the mind, going into the Flow instead aims to completely *occupy* the mind by giving it a rich variety of things to do. When you can feel the energy bubbling inside, smell the Flow like seawater, see the stream of sparkles, hear the *whoosh-whoosh* of the energy, and taste it like pure mountain water in your mouth, you've completely engaged your senses and focused your mind to a keen sharpness; that is, a meditative state. Instead of barking out, "Be quiet!" which causes some busy minds to become even more defiantly noisy, you instead give your mind a sensory to-do list as you focus it on the sensations of your Flow.

Also, unlike traditional meditation, daydreaming is something we all already do (just like night dreaming). It's a vital part of life and fulfills critical functions in our psyches. In essence, Flowdreaming is to daydreaming what lucid dreaming is to dreaming. Both inject conscious direction into the dream or meditative state.

Those practicing meditation should be commended, as it can truly be a challenging discipline to master. If you currently meditate, you're bringing to Flowdreaming the experience of having complete command of your mind and the ability to enter at will into a consciously altered mental state. When Flowdreaming, it may feel odd for you to do exactly the opposite of what you usually do when you enter an altered state—instead of experiencing blankness, you'll be filling the space with your consciously directed "dream." As soon as you get over this odd sense of reversal, you'll probably experience very rich, sharply focused Flowdream imagery and sensations right from the start. Certainly, meditation and Flowdreaming are good practices to do together, as they're complementary in every way.

Q. Can I receive information while Flowdreaming? In other words, can I talk to my Greater Self or obtain guidance?

A. Yes. You may notice from time to time that it feels as if some information is being given to you while you're Flowdreaming—as if a message has been "sent" to you that isn't coming from your own mind. Remember that the process of Flowdreamig involves opening up the conduit, or ascending the vibrational scale, to your Greater Self. If your Greater Self has something to tell you, it will find a way, usually as metaphoric imagery, or perhaps even as a startling sentence that feels as if it were spoken inside your mind. Pay close attention, and be thankful when this occurs. And don't be afraid to ask for clarification if you need it. You can also ask that a situation or event come to you that will reinforce, or validate, the guidance you were given.

The Science Behind the Flow

This chapter picks up where Chapter 2 left off—it will introduce you to more of the philosophy and science behind the Flow, along with what I've discovered through my years of research into what the Flow is and why it works. You see, after my first bungled experience with the process, I embarked on a journey to study all I could about it, to see what, if anything, had already been written about this marvelous place.

What I discovered is that the Flow blends a number of disciplines together, such as turn-of-the-century fundamentals of Jungian psychology; a synthesis of two trends that grew out of the mid-1980s—synchronicity and creative visualization; and today's insights into the meaning of consciousness, transpersonal psychology, systems thinking, and quantum theory. And a number of new disciplines of study are currently developing at a rapid clip, such as biophysics, subtle energy studies, energy medicine, and energy psychology, which also tap in to the Flow field.

These disciplines all have one thing in common: They yield the idea that our mind is not isolated, self-contained, and largely powerless over the events in our life, but is in fact an interconnected, nonlocalized, expansive, and powerful creative force that exists in both time and space as we know it, as well as *outside* of time and space, in a creative, manifestational field that I call the Flow, and which others have called "the cosmic consciousness." As you're now already aware, the mind is both an aspect of the brain as well as something that exists *independently* of it.

That so many disparate disciplines have led toward this conclusion is astonishing. In the scientific world, mind, consciousness, and the fundamental patterns of the Universe itself are increasingly being viewed as inextricably intertwined. Consider Dr. Charles Tart's description of the mind/universe connection as understood in transpersonal psychology, in which he describes the Universe as "an intelligent living organism, in a mind dimension that includes material phenomena as a subset. . . ."[1]

The revolutionary idea that consciousness, or *mind,* can exist both in the brain and independent of the brain in a so-called mind dimension has been gaining ever-wider acceptance, among not only the "old believers" (including parapsychologists and the religious- and spiritual-minded) who always intimated this but had difficulty proving it in the world of Newtonian physics, but also by scientists in the often-overlapping fields of consciousness studies and quantum theory.

From this new perspective, mind is no longer an isolated organ wholly made up of chemical processes and electrical energy—the brain may be, but the mind isn't. Consciousness is therefore freed of our physical bodies, and we're only just learning what the ramifications of such freedom may mean.

Just *where* exactly the mind exists in the energetic spectrum is a hot subject at the moment. For example, Nobel laureate physicist Eugene Wigner, as well as other holist physicists, has suggested that our Universe is endowed with a kind of cosmic consciousness (the Flow), of which our small minds are a part.

Physicist Michio Kaku, cofounder of the string field theory, has put forward the idea that there may be ten or more dimensions in our Universe. This has led other scientists to speculate that the mind could very well be within one of these dimensions. Of course, we have difficulty conceptualizing ten dimensions in the same way that a fish that can only swim side to side and back and forth in a very shallow pond can't understand what *up* means, or that a whole world (or *dimension*, to the fish's way of thinking) exists outside of the surface of the pond.[2] Like that fish, we cling to the idea that our minds exist solely within our brains because we've never had "proof" otherwise—that is, we've never had conscious access "above the pond."

This comes as quite a shock, because in the Newtonian world we've all grown up in, we've been taught that each of our thoughts and memories is essentially a sequenced code of neuropeptides stored in the vast data bank of our brain tissue. Thoughts are derived from electrical impulses between neurons. And flashes of insight; epiphanies; creative bursts; transcendental states; sensations of mystery, awe, or unconditional love; and extrasensory experiences are all explained away as strictly biological responses and the results of humanity's evolutionary path.

So while the way you're making sense of these words right now may feel like an entire-body knowing or understanding, you've actually been taught that it's merely the result of some biological "transformation" of printed words into physical data that's expressed to you as thought and understanding. Because at the heart of things, each thought you have is simply generated by molecules and atoms. The positive and negative charges of protons and electrons are ultimately responsible for the huge, magnificent array of thoughts, beliefs, emotions, understandings, and inspirations you have. You, your sense of who you are, are only the product of the organic chemistry in your brain.

Fortunately, this explanation, which many scientists have acknowledged as being ill-fitting anyway, is giving way to a new understanding, such as that mind may find its home in Kaku's ten- or eleven-dimensional universe, or as Wigner suggests, within a cosmic consciousness. Physicist Fred Alan Wolf has described this consciousness as being as vast and enveloping as an ocean, because "consciousness is everything, it fills the universe."[3]

So your mind, your consciousness, which is existing

partially or wholly within this cosmic ocean, likewise fills the Universe. It is both as isolated as a single drop of seawater in the ocean, and as immense as the ocean itself, since that tiny drop is at the same time a holographic representation of the whole. Quantum theory further suggests that this place—the Flow—has in fact no "here" or "there," but everything that exists, has existed, or has the potential to exist is present at the same place at the same time—in essence, everywhere at once. Like a satellite that beams TV signals, this energy is existing *everywhere* in the air and needs only to be picked up by a receiver: the brain, which is the receiver for the mind. Your biological self "tunes" in different events and possibilities in your life from the infinite possibilities that exist in the Flow. The Flow is where the potentiality of all events is existing now.

Every problem that forms in your life has at the same instance countless potential solutions—only you choose which ones to bring to light. Every time you have a thought, you're creating a new flow of energy. A thought is merely an "invisible action"—and every time you take a physical action, such as shifting this book from your left hand to the right, you're creating a flow of energy that has translated into viewable action.

Whether by thought or action, you've chosen among a million possibilities for this very moment to do what you're doing now. And in any given instant, you have a million new possibilities to choose from. We human beings become forgetful and trap ourselves into the small number of options we appear to see. We become accustomed to the narrow, familiar field of possibilities that we've brought in to surround us, and we "forget" about all the other options on the table.

Translated, this all means that you can imagine your brain to be like a radio receiver or TV. Thought and understanding are broadcast into it from a finer substance (which may or may not be physical) that you can imagine as existing above the surface of the reality "pond." Your brain records data that come in via your senses, *and* it translates data that come from "above the pond," merging input from both to create consciousness.

This quantum link between consciousness and universal energy has arisen because physicists have encountered a number of interesting dilemmas as they've pushed the boundaries of science. For example, one conundrum is that in order to objectively measure a phenomenon, such as a quantum particle, the person looking at it must not "touch" or otherwise disturb it—he or she must maintain distance so as not to "contaminate" the very thing he or she is trying to observe. But this is in fact impossible.

It's been mathematically proven that the person perceiving the particle in essence touches that particle with his or her consciousness—imagine observation as the act of extending one's consciousness to perceive, or "touch," the thing you're perceiving—thereby destroying the objectivity of the observation. Thus, mind and matter are one, because no distance between the two can be achieved. And yet, paradoxically, a division obviously exists.

This observation is strikingly similar to a second peculiarity in quantum theory known as *quantum interconnectedness*. Nick Herbert, Ph.D., describes it well by saying, "[I]n the quantum description of two objects, when two objects briefly interact and then you pull them apart, in the description at least they never come apart; there's a kind of stickiness that connects them together, so they're bound together forever in the theory. They never separate, even though they're not interacting anymore. . . . Bell's theorem proves that this connection . . . actually exists in the real world."[4]

What this suggests is that we must profoundly rethink the idea of our mind's fundamental relationship to our physical reality, because this then means that our mind, existing as it does *both* in the cosmic Flow *and* in our brain—permeating both—therefore touches and has access to everything that is, was, or will be; further, it's *always connected to* whatever it has touched. So does this constant access then extend into being able to *affect* or *change* our physical reality through mind alone?

Directing the physical events in our lives is popularly known today as *manifesting*. This is the idea that consciousness alone can and does affect physical reality, or in simpler terms, one can *think something into existence*. Consider the results from a recent paper by Dean I. Radin and Roger D. Nelson of Princeton University. The two physicists statistically analyzed more than 30 years' worth of controlled, multidisciplinary studies (over 800 of them), in which subjects were asked to mentally affect a testing device so that it produced results outside the realm of chance. Radin and Nelson's conclusion was that it is in fact "possible to predict with some small degree of confidence that anomalous positive (or negative) shifts of distribution means will be observed."[5]

In other words, in more than 800 studies, they noticed a consistent effect where mind—that is, mere thinking—has been able to affect physical reality.

If a person can impact the results of controlled, boring tests by merely *thinking, willing,* or *intending* that these tests go one way or another, then you can imagine the implications if this phenomenon is extended into everyday reality. In your mundane life, what would it mean to you to be able to *will* that you receive the job offer you've always wanted? Or to cause a perfect romantic relationship to come to you? What, really, is the difference between this and changing the output of a mechanical testing device? In both instances, your mind has had to exert influence over matter, and both results are caused by the same fundamental effort. In both cases, the mind, in its ocean (or Flow) of consciousness, has simply reached forward through *intention* to change something. It therefore stands to reason that one's consciousness can direct, or shape, one's reality at will.

Flowdreaming is both a philosophical perspective that some say is decades ahead of our era, as well as a technique to help you explore your creative potential to alter and direct situations in your life. The Flow is really just a metaphor—a tangible image—for this ocean of consciousness, which you can also think of as superfine energy, a manifestational force, a unified field, or an extradimensional "level" or "place" where all things that are, have been, or will be exist. It further helps to think of it as a place where time and space *do not* exist. You can imagine the Flow as the precursor to time and space—the raw stuff that both are made from.

As they say, "No one ages in heaven." In other words, we already take it for granted that there exists a place where time is nonexistent. Time is just a tool that we use here in our three-dimensional world to allow us to move. Without it, we'd be frozen where we are right now, unable to make any movement at all. Time allows us to participate in motion. As soon as we move, we've used the currency of time to get us from the place we were to where we are now. Go ahead and try, right now, to do something without using time to do it—you simply can't. However, being that the Flow is the underlying stuff of the cosmos, the energetic precursor to all physical reality, it's inherently a timeless zone.

When a portion of the Greater You stepped out of this zone into physical reality, you accepted both time and space as the "medium" you'd use for expression of events in a linear way—to experience reality bit by bit, one piece at a time, instead of all at once (much as an artist chooses the "medium" of paint for the expression of his or her ideas onto canvas). The idea of an energetic state where time and place don't exist can be as difficult for us to imagine as it would be to imagine a brand-new color, one that's never been seen before. Try it, and you'll always find that the color is "like" another one you already know—a variation of red, or green, or white, or even clear.

As a side note, when people talk of karma, life paths, predetermined events, or charts set up before we were born, none of that makes sense from a Flow perspective once we get outside of a linear, time-based world like our own. Outside of our physical reality, every event has the potential to exist at once—there is no "past" or "future." Instead, life is evolving and being constantly modified in the *now*. You can see your life as an ever-changing canvas of color, with you as the artist changing and instructing the vision of your future, instant by instant. Only if you think that time controls you do your see your existence as a paint-by-numbers, predetermined lifetime.

In this timeless zone, you'd recognize that every event is being simultaneously created and experienced *by* you and *for* you on multiple levels of reality—you're only tuning to one "frequency" of the experience of you. Setting up a different experience is as easy as changing your mind. This philosophy takes into account our ability to learn and change from our experience, and make moment-by-moment decisions about what to experience so that it stays in alignment with our constant growth, which karma and destiny don't factor in so well.

Mind-boggling as this all seems, this philosophy also means that if you're a believer in past lives, then those lives—indeed all of life itself existing anywhere in the physical Universe—are theoretically happening simultaneously, and through birth we've just opened our eyes to one fragment of it to experience. So while *we* see life through a linear filter that locks us into one time line, in the greater scheme of things, all time is potentially existing right now. This means that parts of you could be existing in multiple lives in multiple times all at once—experiencing everything in the blink of an eye. A part of your consciousness might be embedded in the mind of a medieval knight, another part might be a small girl in futuristic China, another part could be a peasant in revolutionary Russia, and still another part may be reading this right here, right now, in the 21st century.

Because the Greater You exists in a timeless place, what better way to learn than to place itself into multiple physical situations at once, using every event in each life as a learning experience that simultaneously affects all of itself? What more effective way to learn and grow and experience?

To make this idea more clear, imagine this Greater You as a giant energetic Being, and all your physical lives or bodies as gloves. This Being simply puts a piece of itself into many gloves at one time, in one instant. When it's done with a glove, it removes its vibratory energy from it. Death is only viewed as a huge transition from our limited perspective—from the vantage point of the Greater You, it just goes on existing as it always has, except that it has withdrawn its energy from one tiny fragment of physicality. It, itself, doesn't really change. The greater amount of change happened to it through all the billions of experiences that that particular glove accumulated over its physical lifetime—and when added up, they acted to reshape and otherwise affect the Greater You.

The key idea here is that there is no linear sequence, except as we view it here from our earthly perspective. Our stubborn adherence to a linear understanding is what has driven so much philosophy regarding how we "learn lessons" from one life after another, each building upon the last in a slow progression, or that we're on our last life, and so forth. The truth is greater than that.

You see, we're everything at once, and we're choosing to experience only what we want at this given moment. We don't need to "set up events" *before* we're born because every moment the Greater You is fine-tuning and adjusting, according to what it's learning second by second. If something *is* "predestined," it's just been set up by the Greater You to *appear* to arrive at a certain linear time in your life. It could have been planned at any time—even a few seconds before, so to speak, since it comes from a timeless place.

Do you see what enormous power this gives you? You're no longer at the mercy of "working out karma" and "repaying debts" and waiting for that next bad thing to happen to you in retribution for something you did in a past life. While the Greater You may be interested in creating vibrational harmony and symmetry in itself by balancing out energetic situations as they occur, it wouldn't lock itself into a plodding "tit-for-tat" or "an-eye-for-an-eye" driven reality.

Remember the idea of the glove. From our small biological perspective, life is like a one-way mirror: All the rest of the Universe sees us, but when we look back, all we see . . . is our glove.

Flowdreaming is a tool that can help you manifest anything you want in your life. For it to be most effective, however, you might want to study the principles of manifesting further by reading any of the many terrific books on the art. Further study into the fields of quantum theory, Jungian psychology, mind/body studies, energy therapy, creative visualization, and synchronicity also all hold strong similarities to aspects of the Flow. Learning more about these can further your scientific understanding of Flow, and give your Flow experiences a psychological underpinning.

Some of the best writers and teachers on these subjects include Shakti Gawain, Arthur Koestler, Dr. Wayne Dyer, Deepak Chopra, Dr. Charles Tart, Jerry and Esther Hicks, Fritjof Capra, C. G. Jung, Fred Alan Wolf, Jeffery Mishlove, Dean I. Radin, Roger D. Nelson, Nick Herbert, F. David Peat, Rupert Sheldrake, and many others who have all significantly contributed to the understanding of quantum reality and/or how the mind affects our physical reality.

Appendix

Using the CD

The enclosed CD, *Flowdreaming for the Best of Everything*, contains five tracks that will get you started on the Flowdreaming journey. I say "journey" because in my years of performing this process, I've discovered that it's one that's continually evolving. I always say that I'm like a scout or an explorer who's traveled ahead a certain amount and can report back my findings. There's certainly more to discover about this process.

While this CD is an introduction to Flowdreaming, there's never a point at which you'll outgrow any of the Flowdreams on these tracks. That is because as you grow, your experience of each of them will likewise deepen and evolve.

Allow me to discuss each track in depth here.

— Track 1, "An Introduction."

— Track 2, "Exercise 1: Your Emotional Self," is an exercise designed to heighten your awareness of, and control over, your emotional self. Becoming an expert with this track will help you generate the emotional will to create strong, effective Flowdreams.

— Track 3, "Exercise 2: Your Energetic Self," will help you gain awareness about the underlying energy that makes up your body and all things. It should help you become comfortable with thinking of yourself and everything around you as being composed of energy, which will aid you in accepting the core philosophy of Flowdreaming and make the entire process feel more real to you.

For many of you, seeing yourself as made up of energy is easy to do theoretically. But have you ever experienced a hint of how that may *feel?* In this exercise, we'll explore the energetic makeup of our bodies. Sensing even a smidgen of this energy can awaken your entire self to a greater experience of the Flow state. Since the entire concept relies on energy, it makes sense to charge up your own awareness of your energetic self.

We begin by sensing the quantum energy that runs through our bodies, through our meridians or energy pathways. Many alternative-health (especially bioenergetic) practices assess and treat the body's energetic makeup. As a growing field, energy therapies are making up a greater and greater share of new holistic practices. But for the purposes of

Flowdreaming, by getting in touch with your own energetic body, you'll be strengthening your connection to the deeper vibratory levels of your Greater Self. This short exercise introduces you to some of the areas of your body that store and regulate this energy. Practice it whenever you feel low energy levels as a preliminary exercise for Flowdreaming.

— Track 4, "Flowdreaming for the Best of Everything," takes you on a journey of "straight Flow." Its purpose is to reposition you into your own Flow, where everything for your highest good and ease can start working its way into your life. When you play this track, you cede control over life to the Greater You, and allow it to direct your life as it sees fit. Play this track often.

— Track 5, "Flowdreaming for Financial Abundance," seeks to open up the channels to allow more money and prosperity to flow into your life.

— Finally, Track 6, "Flowdreaming for Emotional Fulfillment and Harmonious Relationships," can help you repattern the energies surrounding difficult relationships—both romantically and within your family—so that you again have love and comfort in your life. It can also help you attract new, joy-filled relationships.

I hope you enjoy the process!

Research Resources

The following Websites can guide your further research in the area of consciousness. It is by no means a comprehensive list, but it's a good starting point for those of you interested in reading more about the quantum science that's the basis of Flowdreaming.

Flowdreaming.com
www.flowdreaming.com
To learn more about Flowdreaming, please visit my Website to read more articles about it and hear listening samples of the Flowdreaming CDs available. You can also sign up for the Flowdreaming e-newsletter to get up-to-

the-minute information about Flowdreaming, as well as whatever else is on my mind.

PEAR (Princeton Engineering Anomalies Research)
www.princeton.edu/~pear/
The Princeton Engineering Anomalies Research program conducts research to gain a better understanding of the role of consciousness in physical reality.

Boundary Institute
www.boundaryinstitute.org
This institute studies phenomena associated with consciousness, and ultimately the nature of reality itself.

Society for Scientific Exploration and Journal of Scientific Exploration
www.scientificexploration.org
This organization provides a forum for examining phenomena that are ignored within mainstream science. Their mission statement states that "today's anomaly may become tomorrow's technology."

Rhine Research Center: Institute for Parapsychology
www.rhine.org
The center uses scientific principles to study parapsychology, including telepathy, remote viewing (clairvoyance), precognition, psychokinesis, and the survival of consciousness after death.

Fred Alan Wolf, Physicist
www.stardrive.org/fred.shtml
Dr. Wolf combines quantum physics with studies into the nature of spirit, soul, matter, and self.

Michio Kaku, Theoretical Physicist
www.mkaku.org
As I mentioned previously, Dr. Kaku is the cofounder of string field theory, and is the author of international best-sellers such as *Hyperspace, Visions,* and *Beyond Einstein.* His revelations about the multidimensional nature of our world are truly astonishing.

F. David Peat, Physicist
www.fdavidpeat.com
Dr. Peat is a theoretical physicist whose research into synchronicity as a bridge between mind and matter is particularly interesting.

International Consciousness Research Laboratories
www.icrl.org
International Consciousness Research Laboratories represents scholars in three countries and five academic fields who explore the role of consciousness in physical reality. ICRL was developed by the founders of the Princeton Engineering Anomalies Research (PEAR) laboratory at Princeton University.

Dean Radin, Physicist
www.deanradin.com
Dr. Radin founded the Consciousness Research Laboratory, which conducts scientific research on psychic (or *psi*) phenomena.

The Laboratories for Fundamental Research
www.lfr.org
This site has a link to the Cognitive Sciences Laboratory, which researches anomalous mental phenomena. Their government-sponsored STAR GATE program is well known today.

Endnotes

CHAPTER 7

1. Consciousness: A Psychological, Transpersonal and Parapsychological Approach, Charles T. Tart. *This paper was presented at the Third International Symposium on Science and Consciousness in Ancient Olympia, 4-7 January, 1993.*

2. *Hyperspace: A Scientific Odyssey Through Parallel Universes, Time Warps, and the 10th Dimension,* by Michio Kaku.

3. Transcript from *Thinking Allowed® Conversations on the Leading Edge of Knowledge and Discovery*—*"Physics and Consciousness with Fred Alan Wolf"*—*with Jeffery Mishlove, Ph.D.* © Thinking Allowed Productions.

4. Transcript from *Thinking Allowed® Conversations on the Leading Edge of Knowledge and Discovery*—*"Consciousness and Quantum Reality with Nick Herbert, Ph.D."*—*with Jeffery Mishlove, Ph.D.* © Thinking Allowed Productions.

5. Evidence for Consciousness-Related Anomalies in Random Physical Systems, D. I. Radin, R. D. Nelson. *Foundations of Physics*, Vol. 19, No 12, pp 1499-1514, December 1989.

About the Author

Summer McStravick is the producer/director of HayHouseRadio.com, an Internet radio network parented by Hay House, Inc., the world's leading publisher of self-help titles, which was founded by Louise Hay. In her role as producer, Summer is focused on creating a new kind of talk radio that inspires, enlightens, and uplifts. In addition to producing all of the network's live programming each week, Summer also hosts *The Power of Intention with Dr. Wayne Dyer,* the *Radio for Your Soul Premier Hour* (which showcases new thinkers in the fields of personal growth and whole-body wellness), and her own personal show, *Flowdreaming.*

Flowdreaming introduces listeners to a technique that radically transformed Summer's own life. As a lifelong student of metaphysics and the mind, Summer began spontaneously experiencing the "Flow" in 1999, when she noticed that her family's special "guided daydreaming" technique was transforming into something even more powerful and effective than she'd ever experienced before. Prompted by this phenomenon to study the latest in consciousness research and theoretical physics, over a period of years she refined her family's technique, and her results are now available for the first time ever in a series of CDs that guide the listener through the Flowdreaming process. Today, Summer uses the Flow almost daily in her own life, and also teaches others how to access this important aspect of themselves.

Please feel free to contact Summer anytime to share the successful results of your Flowdreaming experience, as she'd love to hear how the process has worked for you. Summer is also periodically available for lectures and interviews.

Via the Web: **www.flowdreaming.com**
By e-mail: **summer@flowdreaming.com**
By mail:
    Flowdreaming
    P.O. Box 230519
    Encinitas, CA 92024

Hay House Titles of Related Interest

The Amazing Power of Deliberate Intent,
by Esther and Jerry Hicks (The Teachings of Abraham)

Eliminating Stress, Finding Inner Peace (book-with-CD),
by Brian L. Weiss, M.D.

The End of Karma, by Dharma Singh Khalsa, M.D.

Getting in the Gap (book-with-CD),
by Dr. Wayne W. Dyer

Mending the Past and Healing the Future with Soul Retrieval,
by Alberto Villoldo, Ph.D.

Power vs. Force, by David R. Hawkins, M.D., Ph.D.

Silent Power (book-with-CD), by Stuart Wilde

Spirit-Centered Relationships (book-with-CD),
by Gay and Kathlyn Hendricks

◈ ◈ ◈